Richard III by William Shakespeare

The life of William Shakespeare, arguably the most significant figure in the Western literary canon, is relatively unknown.

Shakespeare was born in Stratford-upon-Avon in 1565, possibly on the 23rd April, St. George's Day, and baptised there on 26th April.

Little is known of his education and the first firm facts to his life relate to his marriage, aged 18, to Anne Hathaway, who was 26 and from the nearby village of Shottery. Anne gave birth to their first son six months later.

Shakespeare's first play, The Comedy of Errors began a procession of real heavyweights that were to emanate from his pen in a career of just over twenty years in which 37 plays were written and his reputation forever established.

This early skill was recognised by many and by 1594 the Lord Chamberlain's Men were performing his works. With the advantage of Shakespeare's progressive writing they rapidly became London's leading company of players, affording him more exposure and, following the death of Queen Elizabeth in 1603, a royal patent by the new king, James I, at which point they changed their name to the King's Men.

By 1598, and despite efforts to pirate his work, Shakespeare's name was well known and had become a selling point in its own right on title pages.

No plays are attributed to Shakespeare after 1613, and the last few plays he wrote before this time were in collaboration with other writers, one of whom is likely to be John Fletcher who succeeded him as the house playwright for the King's Men.

William Shakespeare died two months later on April 23rd, 1616, survived by his wife, two daughters and a legacy of writing that none have since yet eclipsed.

Index of Contents
DRAMATIS PERSONAE
ACT I
Scene I - London. A Street
Scene II - The Same. Another Street
Scene III - The Palace
Scene IV - London. The Tower
ACT II
Scene I - London. The Palace
Scene II - The Palace
Scene III - London. A Street
Scene IV - London. The Palace
ACT III
Scene I - London. A Street
Scene II - Before Lord Hastings' House
Scene III - Pomfret Castle

Scene IV - The Tower of London
Scene V - The Tower Walls
Scene VI - The Same
Scene VII - Baynard's Castle
ACT IV
Scene I - Before the Tower
Scene II - London. The Palace
Scene III - The Same
Scene IV - Before the Palace
Scene V - Lord Derby's House
ACT V
Scene I - Salisbury. An Open Place
Scene II - The Camp Near Tamworth
Scene III - Bosworth Field
Scene IV - Another Part of the Field
Scene V - Another Part of the Field
William Shakespeare – A Short Biography
William Shakespeare – A Concise Bibliography
Shakespeare; or, the Poet by Ralph Waldo Emerson
William Shakespeare – A Tribute in Verse

DRAMATIS PERSONAE
ELIZABETH, Queen of King Edward the Fourth
EDWARD, Prince of Wales; afterwards King Edward the Fifth, & RICHARD, Duke of York, Sons to the King
GEORGE, Duke of Clarence, & RICHARD, Duke of Gloucester, afterwards King Richard the Third, Brothers to the King
DUCHESS OF YORK, Mother to King Edward the Fourth, Clarence, and Gloucester
MARGARET, Widow of King Henry the Sixth
A young Son of Clarence
HENRY, Earl of Richmond; afterwards King Henry the Seventh
CARDINAL BOURCHIER, Archbishop of Canterbury
THOMAS ROTHERHAM, Archbishop of York
JOHN MORTON, Bishop of Ely
DUKE OF BUCKINGHAM
DUKE OF NORFOLK
LADY ANNE, Widow of Edward, Prince of Wales, Son to King Henry the Sixth; afterwards married to the Duke of Gloucester
EARL OF SURREY, his Son
EARL RIVERS, Brother to King Edward's Queen
MARQUESS OF DORSET, and LORD GREY, her Sons
LADY MARGARET PLANTAGENET, a young Daughter of Clarence
EARL OF OXFORD
LORD HASTINGS
LORD STANLEY, called also EARL OF DERBY
LORD LOVEL
SIR THOMAS VAUGHAN
SIR RICHARD RATCLIFF

SIR WILLIAM CATESBY
SIR JAMES TYRRELL
SIR JAMES BLOUNT
SIR WALTER HERBERT
SIR ROBERT BRAKENBURY, Lieutenant of the Tower
SIR WILLIAM BRANDON
CHRISTOPHER URSWICK, a Priest
Another Priest
Lord Mayor of London, Sheriff of Wiltshire
TRESSEL and BERKELEY, Gentlemen attending on Lady Anne
Lords, and other Attendants; two Gentlemen, a Pursuivant, Scrivener, Citizens, Murderers, Messengers, Ghosts of those murdered by Richard the Third, Soldiers

SCENE—England.

ACT I

SCENE I. London. A Street

Enter GLOUCESTER, solus

GLOUCESTER
Now is the winter of our discontent
Made glorious summer by this sun of York;
And all the clouds that lour'd upon our house
In the deep bosom of the ocean buried.
Now are our brows bound with victorious wreaths;
Our bruised arms hung up for monuments;
Our stern alarums changed to merry meetings,
Our dreadful marches to delightful measures.
Grim-visaged war hath smooth'd his wrinkled front;
And now, instead of mounting barded steeds
To fright the souls of fearful adversaries,
He capers nimbly in a lady's chamber
To the lascivious pleasing of a lute.
But I, that am not shaped for sportive tricks,
Nor made to court an amorous looking-glass;
I, that am rudely stamp'd, and want love's majesty
To strut before a wanton ambling nymph;
I, that am curtail'd of this fair proportion,
Cheated of feature by dissembling nature,
Deformed, unfinish'd, sent before my time
Into this breathing world, scarce half made up,
And that so lamely and unfashionable
That dogs bark at me as I halt by them;
Why, I, in this weak piping time of peace,
Have no delight to pass away the time,

Unless to spy my shadow in the sun
And descant on mine own deformity:
And therefore, since I cannot prove a lover,
To entertain these fair well-spoken days,
I am determined to prove a villain
And hate the idle pleasures of these days.
Plots have I laid, inductions dangerous,
By drunken prophecies, libels and dreams,
To set my brother Clarence and the king
In deadly hate the one against the other:
And if King Edward be as true and just
As I am subtle, false and treacherous,
This day should Clarence closely be mew'd up,
About a prophecy, which says that 'G'
Of Edward's heirs the murderer shall be.
Dive, thoughts, down to my soul: here
Clarence comes.

Enter CLARENCE, guarded, and BRAKENBURY

Brother, good day; what means this armed guard
That waits upon your grace?

CLARENCE
His majesty
Tendering my person's safety, hath appointed
This conduct to convey me to the Tower.

GLOUCESTER
Upon what cause?

CLARENCE
Because my name is George.

GLOUCESTER
Alack, my lord, that fault is none of yours;
He should, for that, commit your godfathers:
O, belike his majesty hath some intent
That you shall be new-christen'd in the Tower.
But what's the matter, Clarence? may I know?

CLARENCE
Yea, Richard, when I know; for I protest
As yet I do not: but, as I can learn,
He hearkens after prophecies and dreams;
And from the cross-row plucks the letter G.
And says a wizard told him that by G
His issue disinherited should be;
And, for my name of George begins with G,
It follows in his thought that I am he.

These, as I learn, and such like toys as these
Have moved his highness to commit me now.

GLOUCESTER
Why, this it is, when men are ruled by women:
'Tis not the king that sends you to the Tower:
My Lady Grey his wife, Clarence, 'tis she
That tempers him to this extremity.
Was it not she and that good man of worship,
Anthony Woodville, her brother there,
That made him send Lord Hastings to the Tower,
From whence this present day he is deliver'd?
We are not safe, Clarence; we are not safe.

CLARENCE
By heaven, I think there's no man is secure
But the queen's kindred and night-walking heralds
That trudge betwixt the king and Mistress Shore.
Heard ye not what an humble suppliant
Lord hastings was to her for his delivery?

GLOUCESTER
Humbly complaining to her deity
Got my lord chamberlain his liberty.
I'll tell you what; I think it is our way,
If we will keep in favour with the king,
To be her men and wear her livery:
The jealous o'erworn widow and herself,
Since that our brother dubb'd them gentlewomen.
Are mighty gossips in this monarchy.

BRAKENBURY
I beseech your graces both to pardon me;
His majesty hath straitly given in charge
That no man shall have private conference,
Of what degree soever, with his brother.

GLOUCESTER
Even so; an't please your worship, Brakenbury,
You may partake of any thing we say:
We speak no treason, man: we say the king
Is wise and virtuous, and his noble queen
Well struck in years, fair, and not jealous;
We say that Shore's wife hath a pretty foot,
A cherry lip, a bonny eye, a passing pleasing tongue;
And that the queen's kindred are made gentle-folks:
How say you sir? Can you deny all this?

BRAKENBURY
With this, my lord, myself have nought to do.

GLOUCESTER
Naught to do with mistress Shore! I tell thee, fellow,
He that doth naught with her, excepting one,
Were best he do it secretly, alone.

BRAKENBURY
What one, my lord?

GLOUCESTER
Her husband, knave: wouldst thou betray me?

BRAKENBURY
I beseech your grace to pardon me, and withal
Forbear your conference with the noble duke.

CLARENCE
We know thy charge, Brakenbury, and will obey.

GLOUCESTER
We are the queen's abjects, and must obey.
Brother, farewell: I will unto the king;
And whatsoever you will employ me in,
Were it to call King Edward's widow sister,
I will perform it to enfranchise you.
Meantime, this deep disgrace in brotherhood
Touches me deeper than you can imagine.

CLARENCE
I know it pleaseth neither of us well.

GLOUCESTER
Well, your imprisonment shall not be long;
Meantime, have patience.

CLARENCE
I must perforce. Farewell.

Exeunt CLARENCE, BRAKENBURY, and Guard

GLOUCESTER
Go, tread the path that thou shalt ne'er return.
Simple, plain Clarence! I do love thee so,
That I will shortly send thy soul to heaven,
If heaven will take the present at our hands.
But who comes here? the new-deliver'd Hastings?

Enter HASTINGS

HASTINGS
Good time of day unto my gracious lord!

GLOUCESTER
As much unto my good lord chamberlain!
Well are you welcome to the open air.
How hath your lordship brook'd imprisonment?

HASTINGS
With patience, noble lord, as prisoners must:
But I shall live, my lord, to give them thanks
That were the cause of my imprisonment.

GLOUCESTER
No doubt, no doubt; and so shall Clarence too;
For they that were your enemies are his,
And have prevail'd as much on him as you.

HASTINGS
More pity that the eagle should be mew'd,
While kites and buzzards prey at liberty.

GLOUCESTER
What news abroad?

HASTINGS
No news so bad abroad as this at home;
The King is sickly, weak and melancholy,
And his physicians fear him mightily.

GLOUCESTER
Now, by Saint Paul, this news is bad indeed.
O, he hath kept an evil diet long,
And overmuch consumed his royal person:
'Tis very grievous to be thought upon.
What, is he in his bed?

HASTINGS
He is.

GLOUCESTER
Go you before, and I will follow you.

Exit HASTINGS

He cannot live, I hope; and must not die
Till George be pack'd with post-horse up to heaven.
I'll in, to urge his hatred more to Clarence,
With lies well steel'd with weighty arguments;
And, if I fall not in my deep intent,
Clarence hath not another day to live:
Which done, God take King Edward to his mercy,
And leave the world for me to bustle in!
For then I'll marry Warwick's youngest daughter.

What though I kill'd her husband and her father?
The readiest way to make the wench amends
Is to become her husband and her father:
The which will I; not all so much for love
As for another secret close intent,
By marrying her which I must reach unto.
But yet I run before my horse to market:
Clarence still breathes; Edward still lives and reigns:
When they are gone, then must I count my gains.

Exit

SCENE II. The Same. Another Street

Enter the corpse of KING HENRY the Sixth, Gentlemen with halberds to guard it; LADY ANNE being the mourner

LADY ANNE
Set down, set down your honourable load,
If honour may be shrouded in a hearse,
Whilst I awhile obsequiously lament
The untimely fall of virtuous Lancaster.
Poor key-cold figure of a holy king!
Pale ashes of the house of Lancaster!
Thou bloodless remnant of that royal blood!
Be it lawful that I invocate thy ghost,
To hear the lamentations of Poor Anne,
Wife to thy Edward, to thy slaughter'd son,
Stabb'd by the selfsame hand that made these wounds!
Lo, in these windows that let forth thy life,
I pour the helpless balm of my poor eyes.
Cursed be the hand that made these fatal holes!
Cursed be the heart that had the heart to do it!
Cursed the blood that let this blood from hence!
More direful hap betide that hated wretch,
That makes us wretched by the death of thee,
Than I can wish to adders, spiders, toads,
Or any creeping venom'd thing that lives!
If ever he have child, abortive be it,
Prodigious, and untimely brought to light,
Whose ugly and unnatural aspect
May fright the hopeful mother at the view;
And that be heir to his unhappiness!
If ever he have wife, let her he made
A miserable by the death of him
As I am made by my poor lord and thee!
Come, now towards Chertsey with your holy load,
Taken from Paul's to be interred there;

And still, as you are weary of the weight,
Rest you, whiles I lament King Henry's corse.

Enter GLOUCESTER

GLOUCESTER
Stay, you that bear the corse, and set it down.

LADY ANNE
What black magician conjures up this fiend,
To stop devoted charitable deeds?

GLOUCESTER
Villains, set down the corse; or, by Saint Paul,
I'll make a corse of him that disobeys.

GENTLEMAN
My lord, stand back, and let the coffin pass.

GLOUCESTER
Unmanner'd dog! stand thou, when I command:
Advance thy halbert higher than my breast,
Or, by Saint Paul, I'll strike thee to my foot,
And spurn upon thee, beggar, for thy boldness.

LADY ANNE
What, do you tremble? are you all afraid?
Alas, I blame you not; for you are mortal,
And mortal eyes cannot endure the devil.
Avaunt, thou dreadful minister of hell!
Thou hadst but power over his mortal body,
His soul thou canst not have; therefore be gone.

GLOUCESTER
Sweet saint, for charity, be not so curst.

LADY ANNE
Foul devil, for God's sake, hence, and trouble us not;
For thou hast made the happy earth thy hell,
Fill'd it with cursing cries and deep exclaims.
If thou delight to view thy heinous deeds,
Behold this pattern of thy butcheries.
O, gentlemen, see, see! dead Henry's wounds
Open their congeal'd mouths and bleed afresh!
Blush, Blush, thou lump of foul deformity;
For 'tis thy presence that exhales this blood
From cold and empty veins, where no blood dwells;
Thy deed, inhuman and unnatural,
Provokes this deluge most unnatural.
O God, which this blood madest, revenge his death!
O earth, which this blood drink'st revenge his death!

Either heaven with lightning strike the murderer dead,
Or earth, gape open wide and eat him quick,
As thou dost swallow up this good king's blood
Which his hell-govern'd arm hath butchered!

GLOUCESTER
Lady, you know no rules of charity,
Which renders good for bad, blessings for curses.

LADY ANNE
Villain, thou know'st no law of God nor man:
No beast so fierce but knows some touch of pity.

GLOUCESTER
But I know none, and therefore am no beast.

LADY ANNE
O wonderful, when devils tell the truth!

GLOUCESTER
More wonderful, when angels are so angry.
Vouchsafe, divine perfection of a woman,
Of these supposed-evils, to give me leave,
By circumstance, but to acquit myself.

LADY ANNE
Vouchsafe, defused infection of a man,
For these known evils, but to give me leave,
By circumstance, to curse thy cursed self.

GLOUCESTER
Fairer than tongue can name thee, let me have
Some patient leisure to excuse myself.

LADY ANNE
Fouler than heart can think thee, thou canst make
No excuse current, but to hang thyself.

GLOUCESTER
By such despair, I should accuse myself.

LADY ANNE
And, by despairing, shouldst thou stand excused;
For doing worthy vengeance on thyself,
Which didst unworthy slaughter upon others.

GLOUCESTER
Say that I slew them not?

LADY ANNE

Why, then they are not dead:
But dead they are, and devilish slave, by thee.

GLOUCESTER
I did not kill your husband.

LADY ANNE
Why, then he is alive.

GLOUCESTER
Nay, he is dead; and slain by Edward's hand.

LADY ANNE
In thy foul throat thou liest: Queen Margaret saw
Thy murderous falchion smoking in his blood;
The which thou once didst bend against her breast,
But that thy brothers beat aside the point.

GLOUCESTER
I was provoked by her slanderous tongue,
which laid their guilt upon my guiltless shoulders.

LADY ANNE
Thou wast provoked by thy bloody mind.
Which never dreamt on aught but butcheries:
Didst thou not kill this king?

GLOUCESTER
I grant ye.

LADY ANNE
Dost grant me, hedgehog? then, God grant me too
Thou mayst be damned for that wicked deed!
O, he was gentle, mild, and virtuous!

GLOUCESTER
The fitter for the King of heaven, that hath him.

LADY ANNE
He is in heaven, where thou shalt never come.

GLOUCESTER
Let him thank me, that holp to send him thither;
For he was fitter for that place than earth.

LADY ANNE
And thou unfit for any place but hell.

GLOUCESTER
Yes, one place else, if you will hear me name it.

LADY ANNE
Some dungeon.

GLOUCESTER
Your bed-chamber.

LADY ANNE
Ill rest betide the chamber where thou liest!

GLOUCESTER
So will it, madam till I lie with you.

LADY ANNE
I hope so.

GLOUCESTER
I know so. But, gentle Lady Anne,
To leave this keen encounter of our wits,
And fall somewhat into a slower method,
Is not the causer of the timeless deaths
Of these Plantagenets, Henry and Edward,
As blameful as the executioner?

LADY ANNE
Thou art the cause, and most accursed effect.

GLOUCESTER
Your beauty was the cause of that effect;
Your beauty: which did haunt me in my sleep
To undertake the death of all the world,
So I might live one hour in your sweet bosom.

LADY ANNE
If I thought that, I tell thee, homicide,
These nails should rend that beauty from my cheeks.

GLOUCESTER
These eyes could never endure sweet beauty's wreck;
You should not blemish it, if I stood by:
As all the world is cheered by the sun,
So I by that; it is my day, my life.

LADY ANNE
Black night o'ershade thy day, and death thy life!

GLOUCESTER
Curse not thyself, fair creature thou art both.

LADY ANNE
I would I were, to be revenged on thee.

GLOUCESTER
It is a quarrel most unnatural,
To be revenged on him that loveth you.

LADY ANNE
It is a quarrel just and reasonable,
To be revenged on him that slew my husband.

GLOUCESTER
He that bereft thee, lady, of thy husband,
Did it to help thee to a better husband.

LADY ANNE
His better doth not breathe upon the earth.

GLOUCESTER
He lives that loves thee better than he could.

LADY ANNE
Name him.

GLOUCESTER
Plantagenet.

LADY ANNE
Why, that was he.

GLOUCESTER
The selfsame name, but one of better nature.

LADY ANNE
Where is he?

GLOUCESTER
Here.

She spitteth at him

Why dost thou spit at me?

LADY ANNE
Would it were mortal poison, for thy sake!

GLOUCESTER
Never came poison from so sweet a place.

LADY ANNE
Never hung poison on a fouler toad.
Out of my sight! thou dost infect my eyes.

GLOUCESTER

Thine eyes, sweet lady, have infected mine.

LADY ANNE
Would they were basilisks, to strike thee dead!

GLOUCESTER
I would they were, that I might die at once;
For now they kill me with a living death.
Those eyes of thine from mine have drawn salt tears,
Shamed their aspect with store of childish drops:
These eyes that never shed remorseful tear,
No, when my father York and Edward wept,
To hear the piteous moan that Rutland made
When black-faced Clifford shook his sword at him;
Nor when thy warlike father, like a child,
Told the sad story of my father's death,
And twenty times made pause to sob and weep,
That all the standers-by had wet their cheeks
Like trees bedash'd with rain: in that sad time
My manly eyes did scorn an humble tear;
And what these sorrows could not thence exhale,
Thy beauty hath, and made them blind with weeping.
I never sued to friend nor enemy;
My tongue could never learn sweet smoothing word;
But now thy beauty is proposed my fee,
My proud heart sues, and prompts my tongue to speak.

She looks scornfully at him

Teach not thy lips such scorn, for they were made
For kissing, lady, not for such contempt.
If thy revengeful heart cannot forgive,
Lo, here I lend thee this sharp-pointed sword;
Which if thou please to hide in this true bosom.
And let the soul forth that adoreth thee,
I lay it naked to the deadly stroke,
And humbly beg the death upon my knee.

He lays his breast open: she offers at it with his sword

Nay, do not pause; for I did kill King Henry,
But 'twas thy beauty that provoked me.
Nay, now dispatch; 'twas I that stabb'd young Edward,
But 'twas thy heavenly face that set me on.

Here she lets fall the sword

Take up the sword again, or take up me.

LADY ANNE

Arise, dissembler: though I wish thy death,
I will not be the executioner.

GLOUCESTER
Then bid me kill myself, and I will do it.

LADY ANNE
I have already.

GLOUCESTER
Tush, that was in thy rage:
Speak it again, and, even with the word,
That hand, which, for thy love, did kill thy love,
Shall, for thy love, kill a far truer love;
To both their deaths thou shalt be accessary.

LADY ANNE
I would I knew thy heart.

GLOUCESTER
'Tis figured in my tongue.

LADY ANNE
I fear me both are false.

GLOUCESTER
Then never man was true.

LADY ANNE
Well, well, put up your sword.

GLOUCESTER
Say, then, my peace is made.

LADY ANNE
That shall you know hereafter.

GLOUCESTER
But shall I live in hope?

LADY ANNE
All men, I hope, live so.

GLOUCESTER
Vouchsafe to wear this ring.

LADY ANNE
To take is not to give.

GLOUCESTER

Look, how this ring encompasseth finger.
Even so thy breast encloseth my poor heart;
Wear both of them, for both of them are thine.
And if thy poor devoted suppliant may
But beg one favour at thy gracious hand,
Thou dost confirm his happiness for ever.

LADY ANNE
What is it?

GLOUCESTER
That it would please thee leave these sad designs
To him that hath more cause to be a mourner,
And presently repair to Crosby Place;
Where, after I have solemnly interr'd
At Chertsey monastery this noble king,
And wet his grave with my repentant tears,
I will with all expedient duty see you:
For divers unknown reasons. I beseech you,
Grant me this boon.

LADY ANNE
With all my heart; and much it joys me too,
To see you are become so penitent.
Tressel and Berkeley, go along with me.

GLOUCESTER
Bid me farewell.

LADY ANNE
'Tis more than you deserve;
But since you teach me how to flatter you,
Imagine I have said farewell already.

Exeunt LADY ANNE, TRESSEL, and BERKELEY

GLOUCESTER
Sirs, take up the corse.

GENTLEMAN
Towards Chertsey, noble lord?

GLOUCESTER
No, to White-Friars; there attend my coining.

Exeunt all but GLOUCESTER

Was ever woman in this humour woo'd?
Was ever woman in this humour won?
I'll have her; but I will not keep her long.
What! I, that kill'd her husband and his father,

To take her in her heart's extremest hate,
With curses in her mouth, tears in her eyes,
The bleeding witness of her hatred by;
Having God, her conscience, and these bars against me,
And I nothing to back my suit at all,
But the plain devil and dissembling looks,
And yet to win her, all the world to nothing!
Ha! Hath she forgot already that brave prince,
Edward, her lord, whom I, some three months since,
Stabb'd in my angry mood at Tewksbury?
A sweeter and a lovelier gentleman,
Framed in the prodigality of nature,
Young, valiant, wise, and, no doubt, right royal,
The spacious world cannot again afford
And will she yet debase her eyes on me,
That cropp'd the golden prime of this sweet prince,
And made her widow to a woful bed?
On me, whose all not equals Edward's moiety?
On me, that halt and am unshapen thus?
My dukedom to a beggarly denier,
I do mistake my person all this while:
Upon my life, she finds, although I cannot,
Myself to be a marvellous proper man.
I'll be at charges for a looking-glass,
And entertain some score or two of tailors,
To study fashions to adorn my body:
Since I am crept in favour with myself,
Will maintain it with some little cost.
But first I'll turn yon fellow in his grave;
And then return lamenting to my love.
Shine out, fair sun, till I have bought a glass,
That I may see my shadow as I pass.

Exit

SCENE III. The Palace

Enter QUEEN ELIZABETH, RIVERS, and GREY

RIVERS
Have patience, madam: there's no doubt his majesty
Will soon recover his accustom'd health.

GREY
In that you brook it in, it makes him worse:
Therefore, for God's sake, entertain good comfort,
And cheer his grace with quick and merry words.

QUEEN ELIZABETH

If he were dead, what would betide of me?

RIVERS
No other harm but loss of such a lord.

QUEEN ELIZABETH
The loss of such a lord includes all harm.

GREY
The heavens have bless'd you with a goodly son,
To be your comforter when he is gone.

QUEEN ELIZABETH
Oh, he is young and his minority
Is put unto the trust of Richard Gloucester,
A man that loves not me, nor none of you.

RIVERS
Is it concluded that he shall be protector?

QUEEN ELIZABETH
It is determined, not concluded yet:
But so it must be, if the king miscarry.

Enter BUCKINGHAM and DERBY

GREY
Here come the lords of Buckingham and Derby.

BUCKINGHAM
Good time of day unto your royal grace!

DERBY
God make your majesty joyful as you have been!

QUEEN ELIZABETH
The Countess Richmond, good my Lord of Derby.
To your good prayers will scarcely say amen.
Yet, Derby, notwithstanding she's your wife,
And loves not me, be you, good lord, assured
I hate not you for her proud arrogance.

DERBY
I do beseech you, either not believe
The envious slanders of her false accusers;
Or, if she be accused in true report,
Bear with her weakness, which, I think proceeds
From wayward sickness, and no grounded malice.

RIVERS
Saw you the king to-day, my Lord of Derby?

DERBY
But now the Duke of Buckingham and I
Are come from visiting his majesty.

QUEEN ELIZABETH
What likelihood of his amendment, lords?

BUCKINGHAM
Madam, good hope; his grace speaks cheerfully.

QUEEN ELIZABETH
God grant him health! Did you confer with him?

BUCKINGHAM
Madam, we did: he desires to make atonement
Betwixt the Duke of Gloucester and your brothers,
And betwixt them and my lord chamberlain;
And sent to warn them to his royal presence.

QUEEN ELIZABETH
Would all were well! but that will never be
I fear our happiness is at the highest.

Enter GLOUCESTER, HASTINGS, and DORSET

GLOUCESTER
They do me wrong, and I will not endure it:
Who are they that complain unto the king,
That I, forsooth, am stern, and love them not?
By holy Paul, they love his grace but lightly
That fill his ears with such dissentious rumours.
Because I cannot flatter and speak fair,
Smile in men's faces, smooth, deceive and cog,
Duck with French nods and apish courtesy,
I must be held a rancorous enemy.
Cannot a plain man live and think no harm,
But thus his simple truth must be abused
By silken, sly, insinuating Jacks?

RIVERS
To whom in all this presence speaks your grace?

GLOUCESTER
To thee, that hast nor honesty nor grace.
When have I injured thee? when done thee wrong?
Or thee? or thee? or any of your faction?
A plague upon you all! His royal person,—
Whom God preserve better than you would wish!—
Cannot be quiet scarce a breathing-while,
But you must trouble him with lewd complaints.

QUEEN ELIZABETH
Brother of Gloucester, you mistake the matter.
The king, of his own royal disposition,
And not provoked by any suitor else;
Aiming, belike, at your interior hatred,
Which in your outward actions shows itself
Against my kindred, brothers, and myself,
Makes him to send; that thereby he may gather
The ground of your ill-will, and so remove it.

GLOUCESTER
I cannot tell: the world is grown so bad,
That wrens make prey where eagles dare not perch:
Since every Jack became a gentleman
There's many a gentle person made a Jack.

QUEEN ELIZABETH
Come, come, we know your meaning, brother Gloucester;
You envy my advancement and my friends':
God grant we never may have need of you!

GLOUCESTER
Meantime, God grants that we have need of you:
Your brother is imprison'd by your means,
Myself disgraced, and the nobility
Held in contempt; whilst many fair promotions
Are daily given to ennoble those
That scarce, some two days since, were worth a noble.

QUEEN ELIZABETH
By Him that raised me to this careful height
From that contented hap which I enjoy'd,
I never did incense his majesty
Against the Duke of Clarence, but have been
An earnest advocate to plead for him.
My lord, you do me shameful injury,
Falsely to draw me in these vile suspects.

GLOUCESTER
You may deny that you were not the cause
Of my Lord Hastings' late imprisonment.

RIVERS
She may, my lord, for—

GLOUCESTER
She may, Lord Rivers! why, who knows not so?
She may do more, sir, than denying that:
She may help you to many fair preferments,

And then deny her aiding hand therein,
And lay those honours on your high deserts.
What may she not? She may, yea, marry, may she—

RIVERS
What, marry, may she?

GLOUCESTER
What, marry, may she! marry with a king,
A bachelor, a handsome stripling too:
I wis your grandam had a worser match.

QUEEN ELIZABETH
My Lord of Gloucester, I have too long borne
Your blunt upbraidings and your bitter scoffs:
By heaven, I will acquaint his majesty
With those gross taunts I often have endured.
I had rather be a country servant-maid
Than a great queen, with this condition,
To be thus taunted, scorn'd, and baited at:

Enter QUEEN MARGARET, behind

Small joy have I in being England's queen.

QUEEN MARGARET
And lessen'd be that small, God, I beseech thee!
Thy honour, state and seat is due to me.

GLOUCESTER
What! threat you me with telling of the king?
Tell him, and spare not: look, what I have said
I will avouch in presence of the king:
I dare adventure to be sent to the Tower.
'Tis time to speak; my pains are quite forgot.

QUEEN MARGARET
Out, devil! I remember them too well:
Thou slewest my husband Henry in the Tower,
And Edward, my poor son, at Tewksbury.

GLOUCESTER
Ere you were queen, yea, or your husband king,
I was a pack-horse in his great affairs;
A weeder-out of his proud adversaries,
A liberal rewarder of his friends:
To royalize his blood I spilt mine own.

QUEEN MARGARET
Yea, and much better blood than his or thine.

GLOUCESTER
In all which time you and your husband Grey
Were factious for the house of Lancaster;
And, Rivers, so were you. Was not your husband
In Margaret's battle at Saint Alban's slain?
Let me put in your minds, if you forget,
What you have been ere now, and what you are;
Withal, what I have been, and what I am.

QUEEN MARGARET
A murderous villain, and so still thou art.

GLOUCESTER
Poor Clarence did forsake his father, Warwick;
Yea, and forswore himself,—which Jesu pardon!—

QUEEN MARGARET
Which God revenge!

GLOUCESTER
To fight on Edward's party for the crown;
And for his meed, poor lord, he is mew'd up.
I would to God my heart were flint, like Edward's;
Or Edward's soft and pitiful, like mine
I am too childish-foolish for this world.

QUEEN MARGARET
Hie thee to hell for shame, and leave the world,
Thou cacodemon! there thy kingdom is.

RIVERS
My Lord of Gloucester, in those busy days
Which here you urge to prove us enemies,
We follow'd then our lord, our lawful king:
So should we you, if you should be our king.

GLOUCESTER
If I should be! I had rather be a pedlar:
Far be it from my heart, the thought of it!

QUEEN ELIZABETH
As little joy, my lord, as you suppose
You should enjoy, were you this country's king,
As little joy may you suppose in me.
That I enjoy, being the queen thereof.

QUEEN MARGARET
A little joy enjoys the queen thereof;
For I am she, and altogether joyless.
I can no longer hold me patient.

Advancing

Hear me, you wrangling pirates, that fall out
In sharing that which you have pill'd from me!
Which of you trembles not that looks on me?
If not, that, I being queen, you bow like subjects,
Yet that, by you deposed, you quake like rebels?
O gentle villain, do not turn away!

GLOUCESTER
Foul wrinkled witch, what makest thou in my sight?

QUEEN MARGARET
But repetition of what thou hast marr'd;
That will I make before I let thee go.

GLOUCESTER
Wert thou not banished on pain of death?

QUEEN MARGARET
I was; but I do find more pain in banishment
Than death can yield me here by my abode.
A husband and a son thou owest to me;
And thou a kingdom; all of you allegiance:
The sorrow that I have, by right is yours,
And all the pleasures you usurp are mine.

GLOUCESTER
The curse my noble father laid on thee,
When thou didst crown his warlike brows with paper
And with thy scorns drew'st rivers from his eyes,
And then, to dry them, gavest the duke a clout
Steep'd in the faultless blood of pretty Rutland—
His curses, then from bitterness of soul
Denounced against thee, are all fall'n upon thee;
And God, not we, hath plagued thy bloody deed.

QUEEN ELIZABETH
So just is God, to right the innocent.

HASTINGS
O, 'twas the foulest deed to slay that babe,
And the most merciless that e'er was heard of!

RIVERS
Tyrants themselves wept when it was reported.

DORSET
No man but prophesied revenge for it.

BUCKINGHAM

Northumberland, then present, wept to see it.

QUEEN MARGARET
What were you snarling all before I came,
Ready to catch each other by the throat,
And turn you all your hatred now on me?
Did York's dread curse prevail so much with heaven?
That Henry's death, my lovely Edward's death,
Their kingdom's loss, my woful banishment,
Could all but answer for that peevish brat?
Can curses pierce the clouds and enter heaven?
Why, then, give way, dull clouds, to my quick curses!
If not by war, by surfeit die your king,
As ours by murder, to make him a king!
Edward thy son, which now is Prince of Wales,
For Edward my son, which was Prince of Wales,
Die in his youth by like untimely violence!
Thyself a queen, for me that was a queen,
Outlive thy glory, like my wretched self!
Long mayst thou live to wail thy children's loss;
And see another, as I see thee now,
Deck'd in thy rights, as thou art stall'd in mine!
Long die thy happy days before thy death;
And, after many lengthen'd hours of grief,
Die neither mother, wife, nor England's queen!
Rivers and Dorset, you were standers by,
And so wast thou, Lord Hastings, when my son
Was stabb'd with bloody daggers: God, I pray him,
That none of you may live your natural age,
But by some unlook'd accident cut off!

GLOUCESTER
Have done thy charm, thou hateful wither'd hag!

QUEEN MARGARET
And leave out thee? stay, dog, for thou shalt hear me.
If heaven have any grievous plague in store
Exceeding those that I can wish upon thee,
O, let them keep it till thy sins be ripe,
And then hurl down their indignation
On thee, the troubler of the poor world's peace!
The worm of conscience still begnaw thy soul!
Thy friends suspect for traitors while thou livest,
And take deep traitors for thy dearest friends!
No sleep close up that deadly eye of thine,
Unless it be whilst some tormenting dream
Affrights thee with a hell of ugly devils!
Thou elvish-mark'd, abortive, rooting hog!
Thou that wast seal'd in thy nativity
The slave of nature and the son of hell!
Thou slander of thy mother's heavy womb!

Thou loathed issue of thy father's loins!
Thou rag of honour! thou detested—

GLOUCESTER
Margaret.

QUEEN MARGARET
Richard!

GLOUCESTER
Ha!

QUEEN MARGARET
I call thee not.

GLOUCESTER
I cry thee mercy then, for I had thought
That thou hadst call'd me all these bitter names.

QUEEN MARGARET
Why, so I did; but look'd for no reply.
O, let me make the period to my curse!

GLOUCESTER
'Tis done by me, and ends in 'Margaret.'

QUEEN ELIZABETH
Thus have you breathed your curse against yourself.

QUEEN MARGARET
Poor painted queen, vain flourish of my fortune!
Why strew'st thou sugar on that bottled spider,
Whose deadly web ensnareth thee about?
Fool, fool! thou whet'st a knife to kill thyself.
The time will come when thou shalt wish for me
To help thee curse that poisonous bunchback'd toad.

HASTINGS
False-boding woman, end thy frantic curse,
Lest to thy harm thou move our patience.

QUEEN MARGARET
Foul shame upon you! you have all moved mine.

RIVERS
Were you well served, you would be taught your duty.

QUEEN MARGARET
To serve me well, you all should do me duty,
Teach me to be your queen, and you my subjects:
O, serve me well, and teach yourselves that duty!

DORSET
Dispute not with her; she is lunatic.

QUEEN MARGARET
Peace, master marquess, you are malapert:
Your fire-new stamp of honour is scarce current.
O, that your young nobility could judge
What 'twere to lose it, and be miserable!
They that stand high have many blasts to shake them;
And if they fall, they dash themselves to pieces.

GLOUCESTER
Good counsel, marry: learn it, learn it, marquess.

DORSET
It toucheth you, my lord, as much as me.

GLOUCESTER
Yea, and much more: but I was born so high,
Our aery buildeth in the cedar's top,
And dallies with the wind and scorns the sun.

QUEEN MARGARET
And turns the sun to shade; alas! alas!
Witness my son, now in the shade of death;
Whose bright out-shining beams thy cloudy wrath
Hath in eternal darkness folded up.
Your aery buildeth in our aery's nest.
O God, that seest it, do not suffer it!
As it was won with blood, lost be it so!

BUCKINGHAM
Have done! for shame, if not for charity.

QUEEN MARGARET
Urge neither charity nor shame to me:
Uncharitably with me have you dealt,
And shamefully by you my hopes are butcher'd.
My charity is outrage, life my shame
And in that shame still live my sorrow's rage.

BUCKINGHAM
Have done, have done.

QUEEN MARGARET
O princely Buckingham I'll kiss thy hand,
In sign of league and amity with thee:
Now fair befal thee and thy noble house!
Thy garments are not spotted with our blood,
Nor thou within the compass of my curse.

BUCKINGHAM
Nor no one here; for curses never pass
The lips of those that breathe them in the air.

QUEEN MARGARET
I'll not believe but they ascend the sky,
And there awake God's gentle-sleeping peace.
O Buckingham, take heed of yonder dog!
Look, when he fawns, he bites; and when he bites,
His venom tooth will rankle to the death:
Have not to do with him, beware of him;
Sin, death, and hell have set their marks on him,
And all their ministers attend on him.

GLOUCESTER
What doth she say, my Lord of Buckingham?

BUCKINGHAM
Nothing that I respect, my gracious lord.

QUEEN MARGARET
What, dost thou scorn me for my gentle counsel?
And soothe the devil that I warn thee from?
O, but remember this another day,
When he shall split thy very heart with sorrow,
And say poor Margaret was a prophetess!
Live each of you the subjects to his hate,
And he to yours, and all of you to God's!

Exit

HASTINGS
My hair doth stand on end to hear her curses.

RIVERS
And so doth mine: I muse why she's at liberty.

GLOUCESTER
I cannot blame her: by God's holy mother,
She hath had too much wrong; and I repent
My part thereof that I have done to her.

QUEEN ELIZABETH
I never did her any, to my knowledge.

GLOUCESTER
But you have all the vantage of her wrong.
I was too hot to do somebody good,
That is too cold in thinking of it now.
Marry, as for Clarence, he is well repaid,

He is frank'd up to fatting for his pains
God pardon them that are the cause of it!

RIVERS
A virtuous and a Christian-like conclusion,
To pray for them that have done scathe to us.

GLOUCESTER
So do I ever:
Aside
being well-advised.
For had I cursed now, I had cursed myself.

Enter CATESBY

CATESBY
Madam, his majesty doth call for you,
And for your grace; and you, my noble lords.

QUEEN ELIZABETH
Catesby, we come. Lords, will you go with us?

RIVERS
Madam, we will attend your grace.

Exeunt all but GLOUCESTER

GLOUCESTER
I do the wrong, and first begin to brawl.
The secret mischiefs that I set abroach
I lay unto the grievous charge of others.
Clarence, whom I, indeed, have laid in darkness,
I do beweep to many simple gulls
Namely, to Hastings, Derby, Buckingham;
And say it is the queen and her allies
That stir the king against the duke my brother.
Now, they believe it; and withal whet me
To be revenged on Rivers, Vaughan, Grey:
But then I sigh; and, with a piece of scripture,
Tell them that God bids us do good for evil:
And thus I clothe my naked villany
With old odd ends stolen out of holy writ;
And seem a saint, when most I play the devil.

Enter two MURDERERS

But, soft! here come my executioners.
How now, my hardy, stout resolved mates!
Are you now going to dispatch this deed?

FIRST MURDERER

We are, my lord; and come to have the warrant
That we may be admitted where he is.

GLOUCESTER
Well thought upon; I have it here about me.

Gives the warrant

When you have done, repair to Crosby Place.
But, sirs, be sudden in the execution,
Withal obdurate, do not hear him plead;
For Clarence is well-spoken, and perhaps
May move your hearts to pity if you mark him.

FIRST MURDERER
Tush!
Fear not, my lord, we will not stand to prate;
Talkers are no good doers: be assured
We come to use our hands and not our tongues.

GLOUCESTER
Your eyes drop millstones, when fools' eyes drop tears:
I like you, lads; about your business straight;
Go, go, dispatch.

FIRST MURDERER
We will, my noble lord.

Exeunt

SCENE IV. London. The Tower

Enter CLARENCE and BRAKENBURY

BRAKENBURY
Why looks your grace so heavily today?

CLARENCE
O, I have pass'd a miserable night,
So full of ugly sights, of ghastly dreams,
That, as I am a Christian faithful man,
I would not spend another such a night,
Though 'twere to buy a world of happy days,
So full of dismal terror was the time!

BRAKENBURY
What was your dream? I long to hear you tell it.

CLARENCE

Methoughts that I had broken from the Tower,
And was embark'd to cross to Burgundy;
And, in my company, my brother Gloucester;
Who from my cabin tempted me to walk
Upon the hatches: thence we looked toward England,
And cited up a thousand fearful times,
During the wars of York and Lancaster
That had befall'n us. As we paced along
Upon the giddy footing of the hatches,
Methought that Gloucester stumbled; and, in falling,
Struck me, that thought to stay him, overboard,
Into the tumbling billows of the main.
Lord, Lord! methought, what pain it was to drown!
What dreadful noise of waters in mine ears!
What ugly sights of death within mine eyes!
Methought I saw a thousand fearful wrecks;
Ten thousand men that fishes gnaw'd upon;
Wedges of gold, great anchors, heaps of pearl,
Inestimable stones, unvalued jewels,
All scatter'd in the bottom of the sea:
Some lay in dead men's skulls; and, in those holes
Where eyes did once inhabit, there were crept,
As 'twere in scorn of eyes, reflecting gems,
Which woo'd the slimy bottom of the deep,
And mock'd the dead bones that lay scatter'd by.

BRAKENBURY
Had you such leisure in the time of death
To gaze upon the secrets of the deep?

CLARENCE
Methought I had; and often did I strive
To yield the ghost: but still the envious flood
Kept in my soul, and would not let it forth
To seek the empty, vast and wandering air;
But smother'd it within my panting bulk,
Which almost burst to belch it in the sea.

BRAKENBURY
Awaked you not with this sore agony?

CLARENCE
O, no, my dream was lengthen'd after life;
O, then began the tempest to my soul,
Who pass'd, methought, the melancholy flood,
With that grim ferryman which poets write of,
Unto the kingdom of perpetual night.
The first that there did greet my stranger soul,
Was my great father-in-law, renowned Warwick;
Who cried aloud, 'What scourge for perjury
Can this dark monarchy afford false Clarence?'

And so he vanish'd: then came wandering by
A shadow like an angel, with bright hair
Dabbled in blood; and he squeak'd out aloud,
'Clarence is come; false, fleeting, perjured Clarence,
That stabb'd me in the field by Tewksbury;
Seize on him, Furies, take him to your torments!'
With that, methoughts, a legion of foul fiends
Environ'd me about, and howled in mine ears
Such hideous cries, that with the very noise
I trembling waked, and for a season after
Could not believe but that I was in hell,
Such terrible impression made the dream.

BRAKENBURY
No marvel, my lord, though it affrighted you;
I promise, I am afraid to hear you tell it.

CLARENCE
O Brakenbury, I have done those things,
Which now bear evidence against my soul,
For Edward's sake; and see how he requites me!
O God! if my deep prayers cannot appease thee,
But thou wilt be avenged on my misdeeds,
Yet execute thy wrath in me alone,
O, spare my guiltless wife and my poor children!
I pray thee, gentle keeper, stay by me;
My soul is heavy, and I fain would sleep.

BRAKENBURY
I will, my lord: God give your grace good rest!

CLARENCE sleeps

Sorrow breaks seasons and reposing hours,
Makes the night morning, and the noon-tide night.
Princes have but their tides for their glories,
An outward honour for an inward toil;
And, for unfelt imagination,
They often feel a world of restless cares:
So that, betwixt their tides and low names,
There's nothing differs but the outward fame.

Enter the TWO MURDERERS

FIRST MURDERER
Ho! who's here?

BRAKENBURY
In God's name what are you, and how came you hither?

FIRST MURDERER

I would speak with Clarence, and I came hither on my legs.

BRAKENBURY
Yea, are you so brief?

SECOND MURDERER
O sir, it is better to be brief than tedious. Show
him our commission; talk no more.

BRAKENBURY reads it

BRAKENBURY
I am, in this, commanded to deliver
The noble Duke of Clarence to your hands:
I will not reason what is meant hereby,
Because I will be guiltless of the meaning.
Here are the keys, there sits the duke asleep:
I'll to the king; and signify to him
That thus I have resign'd my charge to you.

FIRST MURDERER
Do so, it is a point of wisdom: fare you well.

Exit BRAKENBURY

SECOND MURDERER
What, shall we stab him as he sleeps?

FIRST MURDERER
No; then he will say 'twas done cowardly, when he wakes.

SECOND MURDERER
When he wakes! why, fool, he shall never wake till the judgment-day.

FIRST MURDERER
Why, then he will say we stabbed him sleeping.

SECOND MURDERER
The urging of that word 'judgment' hath bred a kind of remorse in me.

FIRST MURDERER
What, art thou afraid?

SECOND MURDERER
Not to kill him, having a warrant for it; but to be damned for killing him, from which no warrant can defend us.

FIRST MURDERER
I thought thou hadst been resolute.

SECOND MURDERER

So I am, to let him live.

FIRST MURDERER
Back to the Duke of Gloucester, tell him so.

SECOND MURDERER
I pray thee, stay a while: I hope my holy humour will change; 'twas wont to hold me but while one would tell twenty.

FIRST MURDERER
How dost thou feel thyself now?

SECOND MURDERER
'Faith, some certain dregs of conscience are yet within me.

FIRST MURDERER
Remember our reward, when the deed is done.

SECOND MURDERER
'Zounds, he dies: I had forgot the reward.

FIRST MURDERER
Where is thy conscience now?

SECOND MURDERER
In the Duke of Gloucester's purse.

FIRST MURDERER
So when he opens his purse to give us our reward, thy conscience flies out.

SECOND MURDERER
Let it go; there's few or none will entertain it.

FIRST MURDERER
How if it come to thee again?

SECOND MURDERER
I'll not meddle with it: it is a dangerous thing: it makes a man a coward: a man cannot steal, but it accuseth him; he cannot swear, but it cheques him; he cannot lie with his neighbour's wife, but it detects him: 'tis a blushing shamefast spirit that mutinies in a man's bosom; it fills one full of obstacles: it made me once restore a purse of gold that I found; it beggars any man that keeps it: it is turned out of all towns and cities for a dangerous thing; and every man that means to live well endeavours to trust to himself and to live without it.

FIRST MURDERER
'Zounds, it is even now at my elbow, persuading me not to kill the duke.

SECOND MURDERER
Take the devil in thy mind, and relieve him not: he would insinuate with thee but to make thee sigh.

FIRST MURDERER

Tut, I am strong-framed, he cannot prevail with me, I warrant thee.

SECOND MURDERER
Spoke like a tail fellow that respects his reputation. Come, shall we to this gear?

FIRST MURDERER
Take him over the costard with the hilts of thy sword, and then we will chop him in the malmsey-butt in the next room.

SECOND MURDERER
O excellent devise! make a sop of him.

FIRST MURDERER
Hark! he stirs: shall I strike?

SECOND MURDERER
No, first let's reason with him.

CLARENCE
Where art thou, keeper? give me a cup of wine.

SECOND MURDERER
You shall have wine enough, my lord, anon.

CLARENCE
In God's name, what art thou?

SECOND MURDERER
A man, as you are.

CLARENCE
But not, as I am, royal.

SECOND MURDERER
Nor you, as we are, loyal.

CLARENCE
Thy voice is thunder, but thy looks are humble.

SECOND MURDERER
My voice is now the king's, my looks mine own.

CLARENCE
How darkly and how deadly dost thou speak!
Your eyes do menace me: why look you pale?
Who sent you hither? Wherefore do you come?

Both
To, to, to—

CLARENCE

To murder me?

Both
Ay, ay.

CLARENCE
You scarcely have the hearts to tell me so,
And therefore cannot have the hearts to do it.
Wherein, my friends, have I offended you?

FIRST MURDERER
Offended us you have not, but the king.

CLARENCE
I shall be reconciled to him again.

SECOND MURDERER
Never, my lord; therefore prepare to die.

CLARENCE
Are you call'd forth from out a world of men
To slay the innocent? What is my offence?
Where are the evidence that do accuse me?
What lawful quest have given their verdict up
Unto the frowning judge? or who pronounced
The bitter sentence of poor Clarence' death?
Before I be convict by course of law,
To threaten me with death is most unlawful.
I charge you, as you hope to have redemption
By Christ's dear blood shed for our grievous sins,
That you depart and lay no hands on me
The deed you undertake is damnable.

FIRST MURDERER
What we will do, we do upon command.

SECOND MURDERER
And he that hath commanded is the king.

CLARENCE
Erroneous vassal! the great King of kings
Hath in the tables of his law commanded
That thou shalt do no murder: and wilt thou, then,
Spurn at his edict and fulfil a man's?
Take heed; for he holds vengeance in his hands,
To hurl upon their heads that break his law.

SECOND MURDERER
And that same vengeance doth he hurl on thee,
For false forswearing and for murder too:

Thou didst receive the holy sacrament,
To fight in quarrel of the house of Lancaster.

FIRST MURDERER
And, like a traitor to the name of God,
Didst break that vow; and with thy treacherous blade
Unrip'dst the bowels of thy sovereign's son.

SECOND MURDERER
Whom thou wert sworn to cherish and defend.

FIRST MURDERER
How canst thou urge God's dreadful law to us,
When thou hast broke it in so dear degree?

CLARENCE
Alas! for whose sake did I that ill deed?
For Edward, for my brother, for his sake: Why, sirs,
He sends ye not to murder me for this
For in this sin he is as deep as I.
If God will be revenged for this deed.
O, know you yet, he doth it publicly,
Take not the quarrel from his powerful arm;
He needs no indirect nor lawless course
To cut off those that have offended him.

FIRST MURDERER
Who made thee, then, a bloody minister,
When gallant-springing brave Plantagenet,
That princely novice, was struck dead by thee?

CLARENCE
My brother's love, the devil, and my rage.

FIRST MURDERER
Thy brother's love, our duty, and thy fault,
Provoke us hither now to slaughter thee.

CLARENCE
Oh, if you love my brother, hate not me;
I am his brother, and I love him well.
If you be hired for meed, go back again,
And I will send you to my brother Gloucester,
Who shall reward you better for my life
Than Edward will for tidings of my death.

SECOND MURDERER
You are deceived, your brother Gloucester hates you.

CLARENCE

O, no, he loves me, and he holds me dear:
Go you to him from me.

BOTH
Ay, so we will.

CLARENCE
Tell him, when that our princely father York
Bless'd his three sons with his victorious arm,
And charged us from his soul to love each other,
He little thought of this divided friendship:
Bid Gloucester think of this, and he will weep.

FIRST MURDERER
Ay, millstones; as be lesson'd us to weep.

CLARENCE
O, do not slander him, for he is kind.

FIRST MURDERER
Right,
As snow in harvest. Thou deceivest thyself:
'Tis he that sent us hither now to slaughter thee.

CLARENCE
It cannot be; for when I parted with him,
He hugg'd me in his arms, and swore, with sobs,
That he would labour my delivery.

SECOND MURDERER
Why, so he doth, now he delivers thee
From this world's thraldom to the joys of heaven.

FIRST MURDERER
Make peace with God, for you must die, my lord.

CLARENCE
Hast thou that holy feeling in thy soul,
To counsel me to make my peace with God,
And art thou yet to thy own soul so blind,
That thou wilt war with God by murdering me?
Ah, sirs, consider, he that set you on
To do this deed will hate you for the deed.

SECOND MURDERER
What shall we do?

CLARENCE
Relent, and save your souls.

FIRST MURDERER

Relent! 'tis cowardly and womanish.

CLARENCE
Not to relent is beastly, savage, devilish.
Which of you, if you were a prince's son,
Being pent from liberty, as I am now,
if two such murderers as yourselves came to you,
Would not entreat for life?
My friend, I spy some pity in thy looks:
O, if thine eye be not a flatterer,
Come thou on my side, and entreat for me,
As you would beg, were you in my distress
A begging prince what beggar pities not?

SECOND MURDERER
Look behind you, my lord.

FIRST MURDERER
Take that, and that: if all this will not do,

Stabs him

I'll drown you in the malmsey-butt within.

Exit, with the body

SECOND MURDERER
A bloody deed, and desperately dispatch'd!
How fain, like Pilate, would I wash my hands
Of this most grievous guilty murder done!

Re-enter FIRST MURDERER

FIRST MURDERER
How now! what mean'st thou, that thou help'st me not?
By heavens, the duke shall know how slack thou art!

SECOND MURDERER
I would he knew that I had saved his brother!
Take thou the fee, and tell him what I say;
For I repent me that the duke is slain.

Exit

FIRST MURDERER
So do not I: go, coward as thou art.
Now must I hide his body in some hole,
Until the duke take order for his burial:
And when I have my meed, I must away;
For this will out, and here I must not stay.

ACT II

SCENE I. London. The Palace

Flourish. Enter KING EDWARD IV sick, QUEEN ELIZABETH, DORSET, RIVERS, HASTINGS, BUCKINGHAM, GREY, and others

KING EDWARD IV
Why, so: now have I done a good day's work:
You peers, continue this united league:
I every day expect an embassage
From my Redeemer to redeem me hence;
And now in peace my soul shall part to heaven,
Since I have set my friends at peace on earth.
Rivers and Hastings, take each other's hand;
Dissemble not your hatred, swear your love.

RIVERS
By heaven, my heart is purged from grudging hate:
And with my hand I seal my true heart's love.

HASTINGS
So thrive I, as I truly swear the like!

KING EDWARD IV
Take heed you dally not before your king;
Lest he that is the supreme King of kings
Confound your hidden falsehood, and award
Either of you to be the other's end.

HASTINGS
So prosper I, as I swear perfect love!

RIVERS
And I, as I love Hastings with my heart!

KING EDWARD IV
Madam, yourself are not exempt in this,
Nor your son Dorset, Buckingham, nor you;
You have been factious one against the other,
Wife, love Lord Hastings, let him kiss your hand;
And what you do, do it unfeignedly.

QUEEN ELIZABETH
Here, Hastings; I will never more remember
Our former hatred, so thrive I and mine!

KING EDWARD IV
Dorset, embrace him; Hastings, love lord marquess.

DORSET
This interchange of love, I here protest,
Upon my part shall be unviolable.

HASTINGS
And so swear I, my lord

They embrace

KING EDWARD IV
Now, princely Buckingham, seal thou this league
With thy embracements to my wife's allies,
And make me happy in your unity.

BUCKINGHAM
Whenever Buckingham doth turn his hate
On you or yours,

To the QUEEN

but with all duteous love
Doth cherish you and yours, God punish me
With hate in those where I expect most love!
When I have most need to employ a friend,
And most assured that he is a friend
Deep, hollow, treacherous, and full of guile,
Be he unto me! this do I beg of God,
When I am cold in zeal to yours.

KING EDWARD IV
A pleasing cordial, princely Buckingham,
is this thy vow unto my sickly heart.
There wanteth now our brother Gloucester here,
To make the perfect period of this peace.

BUCKINGHAM
And, in good time, here comes the noble duke.

Enter GLOUCESTER

GLOUCESTER
Good morrow to my sovereign king and queen:
And, princely peers, a happy time of day!

KING EDWARD IV
Happy, indeed, as we have spent the day.
Brother, we done deeds of charity;
Made peace enmity, fair love of hate,
Between these swelling wrong-incensed peers.

GLOUCESTER
A blessed labour, my most sovereign liege:
Amongst this princely heap, if any here,
By false intelligence, or wrong surmise,
Hold me a foe;
If I unwittingly, or in my rage,
Have aught committed that is hardly borne
By any in this presence, I desire
To reconcile me to his friendly peace:
'Tis death to me to be at enmity;
I hate it, and desire all good men's love.
First, madam, I entreat true peace of you,
Which I will purchase with my duteous service;
Of you, my noble cousin Buckingham,
If ever any grudge were lodged between us;
Of you, Lord Rivers, and, Lord Grey, of you;
That without desert have frown'd on me;
Dukes, earls, lords, gentlemen; indeed, of all.
I do not know that Englishman alive
With whom my soul is any jot at odds
More than the infant that is born to-night
I thank my God for my humility.

QUEEN ELIZABETH
A holy day shall this be kept hereafter:
I would to God all strifes were well compounded.
My sovereign liege, I do beseech your majesty
To take our brother Clarence to your grace.

GLOUCESTER
Why, madam, have I offer'd love for this
To be so bouted in this royal presence?
Who knows not that the noble duke is dead?

They all start

You do him injury to scorn his corse.

RIVERS
Who knows not he is dead! who knows he is?

QUEEN ELIZABETH
All seeing heaven, what a world is this!

BUCKINGHAM
Look I so pale, Lord Dorset, as the rest?

DORSET
Ay, my good lord; and no one in this presence
But his red colour hath forsook his cheeks.

KING EDWARD IV
Is Clarence dead? the order was reversed.

GLOUCESTER
But he, poor soul, by your first order died,
And that a winged Mercury did bear:
Some tardy cripple bore the countermand,
That came too lag to see him buried.
God grant that some, less noble and less loyal,
Nearer in bloody thoughts, but not in blood,
Deserve not worse than wretched Clarence did,
And yet go current from suspicion!

Enter DERBY

DORSET
A boon, my sovereign, for my service done!

KING EDWARD IV
I pray thee, peace: my soul is full of sorrow.

DORSET
I will not rise, unless your highness grant.

KING EDWARD IV
Then speak at once what is it thou demand'st.

DORSET
The forfeit, sovereign, of my servant's life;
Who slew to-day a righteous gentleman
Lately attendant on the Duke of Norfolk.

KING EDWARD IV
Have a tongue to doom my brother's death,
And shall the same give pardon to a slave?
My brother slew no man; his fault was thought,
And yet his punishment was cruel death.
Who sued to me for him? who, in my rage,
Kneel'd at my feet, and bade me be advised
Who spake of brotherhood? who spake of love?
Who told me how the poor soul did forsake
The mighty Warwick, and did fight for me?
Who told me, in the field by Tewksbury
When Oxford had me down, he rescued me,
And said, 'Dear brother, live, and be a king'?
Who told me, when we both lay in the field
Frozen almost to death, how he did lap me
Even in his own garments, and gave himself,
All thin and naked, to the numb cold night?
All this from my remembrance brutish wrath
Sinfully pluck'd, and not a man of you

Had so much grace to put it in my mind.
But when your carters or your waiting-vassals
Have done a drunken slaughter, and defaced
The precious image of our dear Redeemer,
You straight are on your knees for pardon, pardon;
And I unjustly too, must grant it you
But for my brother not a man would speak,
Nor I, ungracious, speak unto myself
For him, poor soul. The proudest of you all
Have been beholding to him in his life;
Yet none of you would once plead for his life.
O God, I fear thy justice will take hold
On me, and you, and mine, and yours for this!
Come, Hastings, help me to my closet.
Oh, poor Clarence!

Exeunt some with KING EDWARD IV and QUEEN MARGARET

GLOUCESTER
This is the fruit of rashness! Mark'd you not
How that the guilty kindred of the queen
Look'd pale when they did hear of Clarence' death?
O, they did urge it still unto the king!
God will revenge it. But come, let us in,
To comfort Edward with our company.

BUCKINGHAM
We wait upon your grace.

Exeunt

SCENE II. The Palace

Enter the DUCHESS OF YORK, with the two children of CLARENCE

BOY
Tell me, good grandam, is our father dead?

DUCHESS OF YORK
No, boy.

BOY
Why do you wring your hands, and beat your breast,
And cry 'O Clarence, my unhappy son!'

GIRL
Why do you look on us, and shake your head,
And call us wretches, orphans, castaways
If that our noble father be alive?

DUCHESS OF YORK
My pretty cousins, you mistake me much;
I do lament the sickness of the king.
As loath to lose him, not your father's death;
It were lost sorrow to wail one that's lost.

BOY
Then, grandam, you conclude that he is dead.
The king my uncle is to blame for this:
God will revenge it; whom I will importune
With daily prayers all to that effect.

GIRL
And so will I.

DUCHESS OF YORK
Peace, children, peace! the king doth love you well:
Incapable and shallow innocents,
You cannot guess who caused your father's death.

BOY
Grandam, we can; for my good uncle Gloucester
Told me, the king, provoked by the queen,
Devised impeachments to imprison him :
And when my uncle told me so, he wept,
And hugg'd me in his arm, and kindly kiss'd my cheek;
Bade me rely on him as on my father,
And he would love me dearly as his child.

DUCHESS OF YORK
Oh, that deceit should steal such gentle shapes,
And with a virtuous vizard hide foul guile!
He is my son; yea, and therein my shame;
Yet from my dugs he drew not this deceit.

BOY
Think you my uncle did dissemble, grandam?

DUCHESS OF YORK
Ay, boy.

BOY
I cannot think it. Hark! what noise is this?

Enter QUEEN ELIZABETH, with her hair about her ears; RIVERS, and DORSET after her

QUEEN ELIZABETH
Oh, who shall hinder me to wail and weep,
To chide my fortune, and torment myself?

I'll join with black despair against my soul,
And to myself become an enemy.

DUCHESS OF YORK
What means this scene of rude impatience?

QUEEN ELIZABETH
To make an act of tragic violence:
Edward, my lord, your son, our king, is dead.
Why grow the branches now the root is wither'd?
Why wither not the leaves the sap being gone?
If you will live, lament; if die, be brief,
That our swift-winged souls may catch the king's;
Or, like obedient subjects, follow him
To his new kingdom of perpetual rest.

DUCHESS OF YORK
Ah, so much interest have I in thy sorrow
As I had title in thy noble husband!
I have bewept a worthy husband's death,
And lived by looking on his images:
But now two mirrors of his princely semblance
Are crack'd in pieces by malignant death,
And I for comfort have but one false glass,
Which grieves me when I see my shame in him.
Thou art a widow; yet thou art a mother,
And hast the comfort of thy children left thee:
But death hath snatch'd my husband from mine arms,
And pluck'd two crutches from my feeble limbs,
Edward and Clarence. O, what cause have I,
Thine being but a moiety of my grief,
To overgo thy plaints and drown thy cries!

BOY
Good aunt, you wept not for our father's death;
How can we aid you with our kindred tears?

GIRL
Our fatherless distress was left unmoan'd;
Your widow-dolour likewise be unwept!

QUEEN ELIZABETH
Give me no help in lamentation;
I am not barren to bring forth complaints
All springs reduce their currents to mine eyes,
That I, being govern'd by the watery moon,
May send forth plenteous tears to drown the world!
Oh for my husband, for my dear lord Edward!

CHILDREN
Oh for our father, for our dear lord Clarence!

DUCHESS OF YORK
Alas for both, both mine, Edward and Clarence!

QUEEN ELIZABETH
What stay had I but Edward? and he's gone.

CHILDREN
What stay had we but Clarence? and he's gone.

DUCHESS OF YORK
What stays had I but they? and they are gone.

QUEEN ELIZABETH
Was never widow had so dear a loss!

CHILDREN
Were never orphans had so dear a loss!

DUCHESS OF YORK
Was never mother had so dear a loss!
Alas, I am the mother of these moans!
Their woes are parcell'd, mine are general.
She for an Edward weeps, and so do I;
I for a Clarence weep, so doth not she:
These babes for Clarence weep and so do I;
I for an Edward weep, so do not they:
Alas, you three, on me, threefold distress'd,
Pour all your tears! I am your sorrow's nurse,
And I will pamper it with lamentations.

DORSET
Comfort, dear mother: God is much displeased
That you take with unthankfulness, his doing:
In common worldly things, 'tis call'd ungrateful,
With dull unwilligness to repay a debt
Which with a bounteous hand was kindly lent;
Much more to be thus opposite with heaven,
For it requires the royal debt it lent you.

RIVERS
Madam, bethink you, like a careful mother,
Of the young prince your son: send straight for him
Let him be crown'd; in him your comfort lives:
Drown desperate sorrow in dead Edward's grave,
And plant your joys in living Edward's throne.

Enter GLOUCESTER, BUCKINGHAM, DERBY, HASTINGS, and RATCLIFF

GLOUCESTER

Madam, have comfort: all of us have cause
To wail the dimming of our shining star;
But none can cure their harms by wailing them.
Madam, my mother, I do cry you mercy;
I did not see your grace: humbly on my knee
I crave your blessing.

DUCHESS OF YORK
God bless thee; and put meekness in thy mind,
Love, charity, obedience, and true duty!

GLOUCESTER
[Aside] Amen; and make me die a good old man!
That is the butt-end of a mother's blessing:
I marvel why her grace did leave it out.

BUCKINGHAM
You cloudy princes and heart-sorrowing peers,
That bear this mutual heavy load of moan,
Now cheer each other in each other's love
Though we have spent our harvest of this king,
We are to reap the harvest of his son.
The broken rancour of your high-swoln hearts,
But lately splinter'd, knit, and join'd together,
Must gently be preserved, cherish'd, and kept:
Me seemeth good, that, with some little train,
Forthwith from Ludlow the young prince be fetch'd
Hither to London, to be crown'd our king.

RIVERS
Why with some little train, my Lord of Buckingham?

BUCKINGHAM
Marry, my lord, lest, by a multitude,
The new-heal'd wound of malice should break out,
Which would be so much the more dangerous
By how much the estate is green and yet ungovern'd:
Where every horse bears his commanding rein,
And may direct his course as please himself,
As well the fear of harm, as harm apparent,
In my opinion, ought to be prevented.

GLOUCESTER
I hope the king made peace with all of us
And the compact is firm and true in me.

RIVERS
And so in me; and so, I think, in all:
Yet, since it is but green, it should be put
To no apparent likelihood of breach,
Which haply by much company might be urged:

Therefore I say with noble Buckingham,
That it is meet so few should fetch the prince.

HASTINGS
And so say I.

GLOUCESTER
Then be it so; and go we to determine
Who they shall be that straight shall post to Ludlow.
Madam, and you, my mother, will you go
To give your censures in this weighty business?

QUEEN ELIZABETH DUCHESS OF YORK
With all our harts.

Exeunt all but BUCKINGHAM and GLOUCESTER

BUCKINGHAM
My lord, whoever journeys to the Prince,
For God's sake, let not us two be behind;
For, by the way, I'll sort occasion,
As index to the story we late talk'd of,
To part the queen's proud kindred from the king.

GLOUCESTER
My other self, my counsel's consistory,
My oracle, my prophet! My dear cousin,
I, like a child, will go by thy direction.
Towards Ludlow then, for we'll not stay behind.

Exeunt

SCENE III. London. A Street

Enter TWO CITIZENS meeting

FIRST CITIZEN
Neighbour, well met: whither away so fast?

SECOND CITIZEN
I promise you, I scarcely know myself:
Hear you the news abroad?

FIRST CITIZEN
Ay, that the king is dead.

SECOND CITIZEN
Bad news, by'r lady; seldom comes the better:
I fear, I fear 'twill prove a troublous world.

Enter another CITIZEN

THIRD CITIZEN
Neighbours, God speed!

FIRST CITIZEN
Give you good morrow, sir.

THIRD CITIZEN
Doth this news hold of good King Edward's death?

SECOND CITIZEN
Ay, sir, it is too true; God help the while!

THIRD CITIZEN
Then, masters, look to see a troublous world.

FIRST CITIZEN
No, no; by God's good grace his son shall reign.

THIRD CITIZEN
Woe to the land that's govern'd by a child!

SECOND CITIZEN
In him there is a hope of government,
That in his nonage council under him,
And in his full and ripen'd years himself,
No doubt, shall then and till then govern well.

FIRST CITIZEN
So stood the state when Henry the Sixth
Was crown'd in Paris but at nine months old.

THIRD CITIZEN
Stood the state so? No, no, good friends, God wot;
For then this land was famously enrich'd
With politic grave counsel; then the king
Had virtuous uncles to protect his grace.

FIRST CITIZEN
Why, so hath this, both by the father and mother.

THIRD CITIZEN
Better it were they all came by the father,
Or by the father there were none at all;
For emulation now, who shall be nearest,
Will touch us all too near, if God prevent not.
O, full of danger is the Duke of Gloucester!
And the queen's sons and brothers haught and proud:

And were they to be ruled, and not to rule,
This sickly land might solace as before.

FIRST CITIZEN
Come, come, we fear the worst; all shall be well.

THIRD CITIZEN
When clouds appear, wise men put on their cloaks;
When great leaves fall, the winter is at hand;
When the sun sets, who doth not look for night?
Untimely storms make men expect a dearth.
All may be well; but, if God sort it so,
'Tis more than we deserve, or I expect.

SECOND CITIZEN
Truly, the souls of men are full of dread:
Ye cannot reason almost with a man
That looks not heavily and full of fear.

THIRD CITIZEN
Before the times of change, still is it so:
By a divine instinct men's minds mistrust
Ensuing dangers; as by proof, we see
The waters swell before a boisterous storm.
But leave it all to God. whither away?

SECOND CITIZEN
Marry, we were sent for to the justices.

THIRD CITIZEN
And so was I: I'll bear you company.

Exeunt

SCENE IV. London. The Palace.

Enter the ARCHBISHOP OF YORK, young YORK, QUEEN ELIZABETH, and the DUCHESS OF YORK

ARCHBISHOP OF YORK
Last night, I hear, they lay at Northampton;
At Stony-Stratford will they be to-night:
To-morrow, or next day, they will be here.

DUCHESS OF YORK
I long with all my heart to see the prince:
I hope he is much grown since last I saw him.

QUEEN ELIZABETH

But I hear, no; they say my son of York
Hath almost overta'en him in his growth.

YORK
Ay, mother; but I would not have it so.

DUCHESS OF YORK
Why, my young cousin, it is good to grow.

YORK
Grandam, one night, as we did sit at supper,
My uncle Rivers talk'd how I did grow
More than my brother: 'Ay,' quoth my uncle Gloucester,
'Small herbs have grace, great weeds do grow apace:'
And since, methinks, I would not grow so fast,
Because sweet flowers are slow and weeds make haste.

DUCHESS OF YORK
Good faith, good faith, the saying did not hold
In him that did object the same to thee;
He was the wretched'st thing when he was young,
So long a-growing and so leisurely,
That, if this rule were true, he should be gracious.

ARCHBISHOP OF YORK
Why, madam, so, no doubt, he is.

DUCHESS OF YORK
I hope he is; but yet let mothers doubt.

YORK
Now, by my troth, if I had been remember'd,
I could have given my uncle's grace a flout,
To touch his growth nearer than he touch'd mine.

DUCHESS OF YORK
How, my pretty York? I pray thee, let me hear it.

YORK
Marry, they say my uncle grew so fast
That he could gnaw a crust at two hours old
'Twas full two years ere I could get a tooth.
Grandam, this would have been a biting jest.

DUCHESS OF YORK
I pray thee, pretty York, who told thee this?

YORK
Grandam, his nurse.

DUCHESS OF YORK

His nurse! why, she was dead ere thou wert born.

YORK
If 'twere not she, I cannot tell who told me.

QUEEN ELIZABETH
A parlous boy: go to, you are too shrewd.

ARCHBISHOP OF YORK
Good madam, be not angry with the child.

QUEEN ELIZABETH
Pitchers have ears.

Enter a MESSENGER

ARCHBISHOP OF YORK
Here comes a messenger. What news?

MESSENGER
Such news, my lord, as grieves me to unfold.

QUEEN ELIZABETH
How fares the prince?

MESSENGER
Well, madam, and in health.

DUCHESS OF YORK
What is thy news then?

MESSENGER
Lord Rivers and Lord Grey are sent to Pomfret,
With them Sir Thomas Vaughan, prisoners.

DUCHESS OF YORK
Who hath committed them?

MESSENGER
The mighty dukes
Gloucester and Buckingham.

QUEEN ELIZABETH
For what offence?

MESSENGER
The sum of all I can, I have disclosed;
Why or for what these nobles were committed
Is all unknown to me, my gracious lady.

QUEEN ELIZABETH

Ay me, I see the downfall of our house!
The tiger now hath seized the gentle hind;
Insulting tyranny begins to jet
Upon the innocent and aweless throne:
Welcome, destruction, death, and massacre!
I see, as in a map, the end of all.

DUCHESS OF YORK
Accursed and unquiet wrangling days,
How many of you have mine eyes beheld!
My husband lost his life to get the crown;
And often up and down my sons were toss'd,
For me to joy and weep their gain and loss:
And being seated, and domestic broils
Clean over-blown, themselves, the conquerors.
Make war upon themselves; blood against blood,
Self against self: O, preposterous
And frantic outrage, end thy damned spleen;
Or let me die, to look on death no more!

QUEEN ELIZABETH
Come, come, my boy; we will to sanctuary.
Madam, farewell.

DUCHESS OF YORK
I'll go along with you.

QUEEN ELIZABETH
You have no cause.

ARCHBISHOP OF YORK
My gracious lady, go;
And thither bear your treasure and your goods.
For my part, I'll resign unto your grace
The seal I keep: and so betide to me
As well I tender you and all of yours!
Come, I'll conduct you to the sanctuary.

Exeunt

ACT III

SCENE I. London. A Street

The trumpets sound. Enter the young PRINCE EDWARD, GLOUCESTER, BUCKINGHAM, CARDINAL, CATESBY, and others

BUCKINGHAM
Welcome, sweet prince, to London, to your chamber.

GLOUCESTER
Welcome, dear cousin, my thoughts' sovereign
The weary way hath made you melancholy.

PRINCE EDWARD
No, uncle; but our crosses on the way
Have made it tedious, wearisome, and heavy
I want more uncles here to welcome me.

GLOUCESTER
Sweet prince, the untainted virtue of your years
Hath not yet dived into the world's deceit
Nor more can you distinguish of a man
Than of his outward show; which, God he knows,
Seldom or never jumpeth with the heart.
Those uncles which you want were dangerous;
Your grace attended to their sugar'd words,
But look'd not on the poison of their hearts :
God keep you from them, and from such false friends!

PRINCE EDWARD
God keep me from false friends! but they were none.

GLOUCESTER
My lord, the mayor of London comes to greet you.

Enter the LORD MAYOR and his train

LORD MAYOR
God bless your grace with health and happy days!

PRINCE EDWARD
I thank you, good my lord; and thank you all.
I thought my mother, and my brother York,
Would long ere this have met us on the way
Fie, what a slug is Hastings, that he comes not
To tell us whether they will come or no!

Enter HASTINGS

BUCKINGHAM
And, in good time, here comes the sweating lord.

PRINCE EDWARD
Welcome, my lord: what, will our mother come?

HASTINGS
On what occasion, God he knows, not I,
The queen your mother, and your brother York,
Have taken sanctuary: the tender prince

Would fain have come with me to meet your grace,
But by his mother was perforce withheld.

BUCKINGHAM
Fie, what an indirect and peevish course
Is this of hers! Lord cardinal, will your grace
Persuade the queen to send the Duke of York
Unto his princely brother presently?
If she deny, Lord Hastings, go with him,
And from her jealous arms pluck him perforce.

CARDINAL
My Lord of Buckingham, if my weak oratory
Can from his mother win the Duke of York,
Anon expect him here; but if she be obdurate
To mild entreaties, God in heaven forbid
We should infringe the holy privilege
Of blessed sanctuary! not for all this land
Would I be guilty of so deep a sin.

BUCKINGHAM
You are too senseless—obstinate, my lord,
Too ceremonious and traditional
Weigh it but with the grossness of this age,
You break not sanctuary in seizing him.
The benefit thereof is always granted
To those whose dealings have deserved the place,
And those who have the wit to claim the place:
This prince hath neither claim'd it nor deserved it;
And therefore, in mine opinion, cannot have it:
Then, taking him from thence that is not there,
You break no privilege nor charter there.
Oft have I heard of sanctuary men;
But sanctuary children ne'er till now.

CARDINAL
My lord, you shall o'er-rule my mind for once.
Come on, Lord Hastings, will you go with me?

HASTINGS
I go, my lord.

PRINCE EDWARD
Good lords, make all the speedy haste you may.

Exeunt CARDINAL and HASTINGS

Say, uncle Gloucester, if our brother come,
Where shall we sojourn till our coronation?

GLOUCESTER

Where it seems best unto your royal self.
If I may counsel you, some day or two
Your highness shall repose you at the Tower:
Then where you please, and shall be thought most fit
For your best health and recreation.

PRINCE EDWARD
I do not like the Tower, of any place.
Did Julius Caesar build that place, my lord?

BUCKINGHAM
He did, my gracious lord, begin that place;
Which, since, succeeding ages have re-edified.

PRINCE EDWARD
Is it upon record, or else reported
Successively from age to age, he built it?

BUCKINGHAM
Upon record, my gracious lord.

PRINCE EDWARD
But say, my lord, it were not register'd,
Methinks the truth should live from age to age,
As 'twere retail'd to all posterity,
Even to the general all-ending day.

GLOUCESTER
[Aside] So wise so young, they say, do never live long.

PRINCE EDWARD
What say you, uncle?

GLOUCESTER
I say, without characters, fame lives long.
Aside
Thus, like the formal vice, Iniquity,
I moralize two meanings in one word.

PRINCE EDWARD
That Julius Caesar was a famous man;
With what his valour did enrich his wit,
His wit set down to make his valour live
Death makes no conquest of this conqueror;
For now he lives in fame, though not in life.
I'll tell you what, my cousin Buckingham,—

BUCKINGHAM
What, my gracious lord?

PRINCE EDWARD

An if I live until I be a man,
I'll win our ancient right in France again,
Or die a soldier, as I lived a king.

GLOUCESTER
[Aside] Short summers lightly have a forward spring.

Enter young YORK, HASTINGS, and the CARDINAL

BUCKINGHAM
Now, in good time, here comes the Duke of York.

PRINCE EDWARD
Richard of York! how fares our loving brother?

YORK
Well, my dread lord; so must I call you now.

PRINCE EDWARD
Ay, brother, to our grief, as it is yours:
Too late he died that might have kept that title,
Which by his death hath lost much majesty.

GLOUCESTER
How fares our cousin, noble Lord of York?

YORK
I thank you, gentle uncle. O, my lord,
You said that idle weeds are fast in growth
The prince my brother hath outgrown me far.

GLOUCESTER
He hath, my lord.

YORK
And therefore is he idle?

GLOUCESTER
O, my fair cousin, I must not say so.

YORK
Then is he more beholding to you than I.

GLOUCESTER
He may command me as my sovereign;
But you have power in me as in a kinsman.

YORK
I pray you, uncle, give me this dagger.

GLOUCESTER

My dagger, little cousin? with all my heart.

PRINCE EDWARD
A beggar, brother?

YORK
Of my kind uncle, that I know will give;
And being but a toy, which is no grief to give.

GLOUCESTER
A greater gift than that I'll give my cousin.

YORK
A greater gift! O, that's the sword to it.

GLOUCESTER
A gentle cousin, were it light enough.

YORK
O, then, I see, you will part but with light gifts;
In weightier things you'll say a beggar nay.

GLOUCESTER
It is too heavy for your grace to wear.

YORK
I weigh it lightly, were it heavier.

GLOUCESTER
What, would you have my weapon, little lord?

YORK
I would, that I might thank you as you call me.

GLOUCESTER
How?

YORK
Little.

PRINCE EDWARD
My Lord of York will still be cross in talk:
Uncle, your grace knows how to bear with him.

YORK
You mean, to bear me, not to bear with me:
Uncle, my brother mocks both you and me;
Because that I am little, like an ape,
He thinks that you should bear me on your shoulders.

BUCKINGHAM

With what a sharp-provided wit he reasons!
To mitigate the scorn he gives his uncle,
He prettily and aptly taunts himself:
So cunning and so young is wonderful.

GLOUCESTER
My lord, will't please you pass along?
Myself and my good cousin Buckingham
Will to your mother, to entreat of her
To meet you at the Tower and welcome you.

YORK
What, will you go unto the Tower, my lord?

PRINCE EDWARD
My lord protector needs will have it so.

YORK
I shall not sleep in quiet at the Tower.

GLOUCESTER
Why, what should you fear?

YORK
Marry, my uncle Clarence' angry ghost:
My grandam told me he was murdered there.

PRINCE EDWARD
I fear no uncles dead.

GLOUCESTER
Nor none that live, I hope.

PRINCE EDWARD
An if they live, I hope I need not fear.
But come, my lord; and with a heavy heart,
Thinking on them, go I unto the Tower.

A Sennet.

Exeunt all but GLOUCESTER, BUCKINGHAM and CATESBY

BUCKINGHAM
Think you, my lord, this little prating York
Was not incensed by his subtle mother
To taunt and scorn you thus opprobriously?

GLOUCESTER
No doubt, no doubt; O, 'tis a parlous boy;
Bold, quick, ingenious, forward, capable
He is all the mother's, from the top to toe.

BUCKINGHAM
Well, let them rest. Come hither, Catesby.
Thou art sworn as deeply to effect what we intend
As closely to conceal what we impart:
Thou know'st our reasons urged upon the way;
What think'st thou? is it not an easy matter
To make William Lord Hastings of our mind,
For the instalment of this noble duke
In the seat royal of this famous isle?

CATESBY
He for his father's sake so loves the prince,
That he will not be won to aught against him.

BUCKINGHAM
What think'st thou, then, of Stanley? what will he?

CATESBY
He will do all in all as Hastings doth.

BUCKINGHAM
Well, then, no more but this: go, gentle Catesby,
And, as it were far off sound thou Lord Hastings,
How doth he stand affected to our purpose;
And summon him to-morrow to the Tower,
To sit about the coronation.
If thou dost find him tractable to us,
Encourage him, and show him all our reasons:
If he be leaden, icy-cold, unwilling,
Be thou so too; and so break off your talk,
And give us notice of his inclination:
For we to-morrow hold divided councils,
Wherein thyself shalt highly be employ'd.

GLOUCESTER
Commend me to Lord William: tell him, Catesby,
His ancient knot of dangerous adversaries
To-morrow are let blood at Pomfret-castle;
And bid my friend, for joy of this good news,
Give mistress Shore one gentle kiss the more.

BUCKINGHAM
Good Catesby, go, effect this business soundly.

CATESBY
My good lords both, with all the heed I may.

GLOUCESTER
Shall we hear from you, Catesby, ere we sleep?

CATESBY
You shall, my lord.

GLOUCESTER
At Crosby Place, there shall you find us both.

Exit CATESBY

BUCKINGHAM
Now, my lord, what shall we do, if we perceive
Lord Hastings will not yield to our complots?

GLOUCESTER
Chop off his head, man; somewhat we will do:
And, look, when I am king, claim thou of me
The earldom of Hereford, and the moveables
Whereof the king my brother stood possess'd.

BUCKINGHAM
I'll claim that promise at your grace's hands.

GLOUCESTER
And look to have it yielded with all willingness.
Come, let us sup betimes, that afterwards
We may digest our complots in some form.

Exeunt

SCENE II. Before Lord Hastings' House

Enter a MESSENGER

MESSENGER
What, ho! my lord!

HASTINGS
[Within] Who knocks at the door?

MESSENGER
A messenger from the Lord Stanley.

Enter HASTINGS

HASTINGS
What is't o'clock?

MESSENGER
Upon the stroke of four.

HASTINGS
Cannot thy master sleep these tedious nights?

MESSENGER
So it should seem by that I have to say.
First, he commends him to your noble lordship.

HASTINGS
And then?

MESSENGER
And then he sends you word
He dreamt to-night the boar had razed his helm:
Besides, he says there are two councils held;
And that may be determined at the one
which may make you and him to rue at the other.
Therefore he sends to know your lordship's pleasure,
If presently you will take horse with him,
And with all speed post with him toward the north,
To shun the danger that his soul divines.

HASTINGS
Go, fellow, go, return unto thy lord;
Bid him not fear the separated councils
His honour and myself are at the one,
And at the other is my servant Catesby
Where nothing can proceed that toucheth us
Whereof I shall not have intelligence.
Tell him his fears are shallow, wanting instance:
And for his dreams, I wonder he is so fond
To trust the mockery of unquiet slumbers
To fly the boar before the boar pursues,
Were to incense the boar to follow us
And make pursuit where he did mean no chase.
Go, bid thy master rise and come to me
And we will both together to the Tower,
Where, he shall see, the boar will use us kindly.

MESSENGER
My gracious lord, I'll tell him what you say.

Exit

Enter CATESBY

CATESBY
Many good morrows to my noble lord!

HASTINGS
Good morrow, Catesby; you are early stirring
What news, what news, in this our tottering state?

CATESBY
It is a reeling world, indeed, my lord;
And I believe twill never stand upright
Tim Richard wear the garland of the realm.

HASTINGS
How! wear the garland! dost thou mean the crown?

CATESBY
Ay, my good lord.

HASTINGS
I'll have this crown of mine cut from my shoulders
Ere I will see the crown so foul misplaced.
But canst thou guess that he doth aim at it?

CATESBY
Ay, on my life; and hopes to find forward
Upon his party for the gain thereof:
And thereupon he sends you this good news,
That this same very day your enemies,
The kindred of the queen, must die at Pomfret.

HASTINGS
Indeed, I am no mourner for that news,
Because they have been still mine enemies:
But, that I'll give my voice on Richard's side,
To bar my master's heirs in true descent,
God knows I will not do it, to the death.

CATESBY
God keep your lordship in that gracious mind!

HASTINGS
But I shall laugh at this a twelve-month hence,
That they who brought me in my master's hate
I live to look upon their tragedy.
I tell thee, Catesby—

CATESBY
What, my lord?

HASTINGS
Ere a fortnight make me elder,
I'll send some packing that yet think not on it.

CATESBY
'Tis a vile thing to die, my gracious lord,
When men are unprepared and look not for it.

HASTINGS
O monstrous, monstrous! and so falls it out
With Rivers, Vaughan, Grey: and so 'twill do
With some men else, who think themselves as safe
As thou and I; who, as thou know'st, are dear
To princely Richard and to Buckingham.

CATESBY
The princes both make high account of you;
Aside
For they account his head upon the bridge.

HASTINGS
I know they do; and I have well deserved it.

Enter STANLEY

Come on, come on; where is your boar-spear, man?
Fear you the boar, and go so unprovided?

STANLEY
My lord, good morrow; good morrow, Catesby:
You may jest on, but, by the holy rood,
I do not like these several councils, I.

HASTINGS
My lord,
I hold my life as dear as you do yours;
And never in my life, I do protest,
Was it more precious to me than 'tis now:
Think you, but that I know our state secure,
I would be so triumphant as I am?

STANLEY
The lords at Pomfret, when they rode from London,
Were jocund, and supposed their state was sure,
And they indeed had no cause to mistrust;
But yet, you see how soon the day o'ercast.
This sudden stag of rancour I misdoubt:
Pray God, I say, I prove a needless coward!
What, shall we toward the Tower? the day is spent.

HASTINGS
Come, come, have with you. Wot you what, my lord?
To-day the lords you talk of are beheaded.

LORD STANLEY
They, for their truth, might better wear their heads
Than some that have accused them wear their hats.
But come, my lord, let us away.

Enter a PURSUIVANT

HASTINGS
Go on before; I'll talk with this good fellow.

Exeunt STANLEY and CATESBY

How now, sirrah! how goes the world with thee?

PURSUIVANT
The better that your lordship please to ask.

HASTINGS
I tell thee, man, 'tis better with me now
Than when I met thee last where now we meet:
Then was I going prisoner to the Tower,
By the suggestion of the queen's allies;
But now, I tell thee—keep it to thyself—
This day those enemies are put to death,
And I in better state than e'er I was.

PURSUIVANT
God hold it, to your honour's good content!

HASTINGS
Gramercy, fellow: there, drink that for me.

Throws him his purse

PURSUIVANT
God save your lordship!

Exit

Enter a PRIEST

PRIEST
Well met, my lord; I am glad to see your honour.

HASTINGS
I thank thee, good Sir John, with all my heart.
I am in your debt for your last exercise;
Come the next Sabbath, and I will content you.
He whispers in his ear

Enter BUCKINGHAM

BUCKINGHAM
What, talking with a priest, lord chamberlain?
Your friends at Pomfret, they do need the priest;
Your honour hath no shriving work in hand.

HASTINGS
Good faith, and when I met this holy man,
Those men you talk of came into my mind.
What, go you toward the Tower?

BUCKINGHAM
I do, my lord; but long I shall not stay
I shall return before your lordship thence.

HASTINGS
'Tis like enough, for I stay dinner there.

BUCKINGHAM
[Aside] And supper too, although thou know'st it not.
Come, will you go?

HASTINGS
I'll wait upon your lordship.

Exeunt

SCENE III. Pomfret Castle

Enter RATCLIFF, with halberds, carrying RIVERS, GREY, and VAUGHAN to death

RATCLIFF
Come, bring forth the prisoners.

RIVERS
Sir Richard Ratcliff, let me tell thee this:
To-day shalt thou behold a subject die
For truth, for duty, and for loyalty.

GREY
God keep the prince from all the pack of you!
A knot you are of damned blood-suckers!

VAUGHAN
You live that shall cry woe for this after.

RATCLIFF
Dispatch; the limit of your lives is out.

RIVERS
O Pomfret, Pomfret! O thou bloody prison,
Fatal and ominous to noble peers!
Within the guilty closure of thy walls
Richard the second here was hack'd to death;

And, for more slander to thy dismal seat,
We give thee up our guiltless blood to drink.

GREY
Now Margaret's curse is fall'n upon our heads,
For standing by when Richard stabb'd her son.

RIVERS
Then cursed she Hastings, then cursed she Buckingham,
Then cursed she Richard. O, remember, God
To hear her prayers for them, as now for us
And for my sister and her princely sons,
Be satisfied, dear God, with our true blood,
Which, as thou know'st, unjustly must be spilt.

RATCLIFF
Make haste; the hour of death is expiate.

RIVERS
Come, Grey, come, Vaughan, let us all embrace:
And take our leave, until we meet in heaven.

Exeunt

SCENE IV. The Tower of London

Enter BUCKINGHAM, DERBY, HASTINGS, the BISHOP OF ELY, RATCLIFF, LOVEL, with others, and take their seats at a table

HASTINGS
My lords, at once: the cause why we are met
Is, to determine of the coronation.
In God's name, speak: when is the royal day?

BUCKINGHAM
Are all things fitting for that royal time?

DERBY
It is, and wants but nomination.

BISHOP OF ELY
To-morrow, then, I judge a happy day.

BUCKINGHAM
Who knows the lord protector's mind herein?
Who is most inward with the royal duke?

BISHOP OF ELY
Your grace, we think, should soonest know his mind.

BUCKINGHAM
Who, I, my lord I we know each other's faces,
But for our hearts, he knows no more of mine,
Than I of yours;
Nor I no more of his, than you of mine.
Lord Hastings, you and he are near in love.

HASTINGS
I thank his grace, I know he loves me well;
But, for his purpose in the coronation.
I have not sounded him, nor he deliver'd
His gracious pleasure any way therein:
But you, my noble lords, may name the time;
And in the duke's behalf I'll give my voice,
Which, I presume, he'll take in gentle part.

Enter GLOUCESTER

BISHOP OF ELY
Now in good time, here comes the duke himself.

GLOUCESTER
My noble lords and cousins all, good morrow.
I have been long a sleeper; but, I hope,
My absence doth neglect no great designs,
Which by my presence might have been concluded.

BUCKINGHAM
Had not you come upon your cue, my lord
William Lord Hastings had pronounced your part,—
I mean, your voice,—for crowning of the king.

GLOUCESTER
Than my Lord Hastings no man might be bolder;
His lordship knows me well, and loves me well.

HASTINGS
I thank your grace.

GLOUCESTER
My lord of Ely!

BISHOP OF ELY
My lord?

GLOUCESTER
When I was last in Holborn,
I saw good strawberries in your garden there
I do beseech you send for some of them.

BISHOP OF ELY
Marry, and will, my lord, with all my heart.

Exit

GLOUCESTER
Cousin of Buckingham, a word with you.

Drawing him aside

Catesby hath sounded Hastings in our business,
And finds the testy gentleman so hot,
As he will lose his head ere give consent
His master's son, as worshipful as he terms it,
Shall lose the royalty of England's throne.

BUCKINGHAM
Withdraw you hence, my lord, I'll follow you.

Exit GLOUCESTER, BUCKINGHAM following

DERBY
We have not yet set down this day of triumph.
To-morrow, in mine opinion, is too sudden;
For I myself am not so well provided
As else I would be, were the day prolong'd.

Re-enter BISHOP OF ELY

BISHOP OF ELY
Where is my lord protector? I have sent for these
strawberries.

HASTINGS
His grace looks cheerfully and smooth to-day;
There's some conceit or other likes him well,
When he doth bid good morrow with such a spirit.
I think there's never a man in Christendom
That can less hide his love or hate than he;
For by his face straight shall you know his heart.

DERBY
What of his heart perceive you in his face
By any likelihood he show'd to-day?

HASTINGS
Marry, that with no man here he is offended;
For, were he, he had shown it in his looks.

DERBY
I pray God he be not, I say.

Re-enter GLOUCESTER and BUCKINGHAM

GLOUCESTER
I pray you all, tell me what they deserve
That do conspire my death with devilish plots
Of damned witchcraft, and that have prevail'd
Upon my body with their hellish charms?

HASTINGS
The tender love I bear your grace, my lord,
Makes me most forward in this noble presence
To doom the offenders, whatsoever they be
I say, my lord, they have deserved death.

GLOUCESTER
Then be your eyes the witness of this ill:
See how I am bewitch'd; behold mine arm
Is, like a blasted sapling, wither'd up:
And this is Edward's wife, that monstrous witch,
Consorted with that harlot strumpet Shore,
That by their witchcraft thus have marked me.

HASTINGS
If they have done this thing, my gracious lord—

GLOUCESTER
If I thou protector of this damned strumpet—
Tellest thou me of 'ifs'? Thou art a traitor:
Off with his head! Now, by Saint Paul I swear,
I will not dine until I see the same.
Lovel and Ratcliff, look that it be done:
The rest, that love me, rise and follow me.

Exeunt all but HASTINGS, RATCLIFF, and LOVEL

HASTINGS
Woe, woe for England! not a whit for me;
For I, too fond, might have prevented this.
Stanley did dream the boar did raze his helm;
But I disdain'd it, and did scorn to fly:
Three times to-day my foot-cloth horse did stumble,
And startled, when he look'd upon the Tower,
As loath to bear me to the slaughter-house.
O, now I want the priest that spake to me:
I now repent I told the pursuivant
As 'twere triumphing at mine enemies,
How they at Pomfret bloodily were butcher'd,
And I myself secure in grace and favour.
O Margaret, Margaret, now thy heavy curse
Is lighted on poor Hastings' wretched head!

RATCLIFF
Dispatch, my lord; the duke would be at dinner:
Make a short shrift; he longs to see your head.

HASTINGS
O momentary grace of mortal men,
Which we more hunt for than the grace of God!
Who builds his hopes in air of your good looks,
Lives like a drunken sailor on a mast,
Ready, with every nod, to tumble down
Into the fatal bowels of the deep.

LOVEL
Come, come, dispatch; 'tis bootless to exclaim.

HASTINGS
O bloody Richard! miserable England!
I prophesy the fearful'st time to thee
That ever wretched age hath look'd upon.
Come, lead me to the block; bear him my head.
They smile at me that shortly shall be dead.

Exeunt

SCENE V. The Tower Walls

Enter GLOUCESTER and BUCKINGHAM, in rotten armour, marvellous ill-favoured

GLOUCESTER
Come, cousin, canst thou quake, and change thy colour,
Murder thy breath in the middle of a word,
And then begin again, and stop again,
As if thou wert distraught and mad with terror?

BUCKINGHAM
Tut, I can counterfeit the deep tragedian;
Speak and look back, and pry on every side,
Tremble and start at wagging of a straw,
Intending deep suspicion: ghastly looks
Are at my service, like enforced smiles;
And both are ready in their offices,
At any time, to grace my stratagems.
But what, is Catesby gone?

GLOUCESTER
He is; and, see, he brings the mayor along.

Enter the LORD MAYOR and CATESBY

BUCKINGHAM
Lord mayor—

GLOUCESTER
Look to the drawbridge there!

BUCKINGHAM
Hark! a drum.

GLOUCESTER
Catesby, o'erlook the walls.

BUCKINGHAM
Lord mayor, the reason we have sent—

GLOUCESTER
Look back, defend thee, here are enemies.

BUCKINGHAM
God and our innocency defend and guard us!

GLOUCESTER
Be patient, they are friends, Ratcliff and Lovel.

Enter LOVEL and RATCLIFF, with HASTINGS' head

LOVEL
Here is the head of that ignoble traitor,
The dangerous and unsuspected Hastings.

GLOUCESTER
So dear I loved the man, that I must weep.
I took him for the plainest harmless creature
That breathed upon this earth a Christian;
Made him my book wherein my soul recorded
The history of all her secret thoughts:
So smooth he daub'd his vice with show of virtue,
That, his apparent open guilt omitted,
I mean, his conversation with Shore's wife,
He lived from all attainder of suspect.

BUCKINGHAM
Well, well, he was the covert'st shelter'd traitor
That ever lived.
Would you imagine, or almost believe,
Were't not that, by great preservation,
We live to tell it you, the subtle traitor
This day had plotted, in the council-house
To murder me and my good Lord of Gloucester?

LORD MAYOR
What, had he so?

GLOUCESTER
What, think You we are Turks or infidels?
Or that we would, against the form of law,
Proceed thus rashly to the villain's death,
But that the extreme peril of the case,
The peace of England and our persons' safety,
Enforced us to this execution?

LORD MAYOR
Now, fair befall you! he deserved his death;
And you my good lords, both have well proceeded,
To warn false traitors from the like attempts.
I never look'd for better at his hands,
After he once fell in with Mistress Shore.

GLOUCESTER
Yet had not we determined he should die,
Until your lordship came to see his death;
Which now the loving haste of these our friends,
Somewhat against our meaning, have prevented:
Because, my lord, we would have had you heard
The traitor speak, and timorously confess
The manner and the purpose of his treason;
That you might well have signified the same
Unto the citizens, who haply may
Misconstrue us in him and wail his death.

LORD MAYOR
But, my good lord, your grace's word shall serve,
As well as I had seen and heard him speak
And doubt you not, right noble princes both,
But I'll acquaint our duteous citizens
With all your just proceedings in this cause.

GLOUCESTER
And to that end we wish'd your lord-ship here,
To avoid the carping censures of the world.

BUCKINGHAM
But since you come too late of our intents,
Yet witness what you hear we did intend:
And so, my good lord mayor, we bid farewell.

Exit LORD MAYOR

GLOUCESTER
Go, after, after, cousin Buckingham.
The mayor towards Guildhall hies him in all post:

There, at your meet'st advantage of the time,
Infer the bastardy of Edward's children:
Tell them how Edward put to death a citizen,
Only for saying he would make his son
Heir to the crown; meaning indeed his house,
Which, by the sign thereof was termed so.
Moreover, urge his hateful luxury
And bestial appetite in change of lust;
Which stretched to their servants, daughters, wives,
Even where his lustful eye or savage heart,
Without control, listed to make his prey.
Nay, for a need, thus far come near my person:
Tell them, when that my mother went with child
Of that unsatiate Edward, noble York
My princely father then had wars in France
And, by just computation of the time,
Found that the issue was not his begot;
Which well appeared in his lineaments,
Being nothing like the noble duke my father:
But touch this sparingly, as 'twere far off,
Because you know, my lord, my mother lives.

BUCKINGHAM
Fear not, my lord, I'll play the orator
As if the golden fee for which I plead
Were for myself: and so, my lord, adieu.

GLOUCESTER
If you thrive well, bring them to Baynard's Castle;
Where you shall find me well accompanied
With reverend fathers and well-learned bishops.

BUCKINGHAM
I go: and towards three or four o'clock
Look for the news that the Guildhall affords.

Exit BUCKINGHAM

GLOUCESTER
Go, Lovel, with all speed to Doctor Shaw;

To CATESBY

Go thou to Friar Penker; bid them both
Meet me within this hour at Baynard's Castle.

Exeunt all but GLOUCESTER

Now will I in, to take some privy order,
To draw the brats of Clarence out of sight;

And to give notice, that no manner of person
At any time have recourse unto the princes.

Exit

SCENE VI. The Same

Enter a SCRIVENER, with a paper in his hand

SCRIVENER
This is the indictment of the good Lord Hastings;
Which in a set hand fairly is engross'd,
That it may be this day read over in Paul's.
And mark how well the sequel hangs together:
Eleven hours I spent to write it over,
For yesternight by Catesby was it brought me;
The precedent was full as long a-doing:
And yet within these five hours lived Lord Hastings,
Untainted, unexamined, free, at liberty
Here's a good world the while! Why who's so gross,
That seeth not this palpable device?
Yet who's so blind, but says he sees it not?
Bad is the world; and all will come to nought,
When such bad dealings must be seen in thought.

Exit

SCENE VII. Baynard's Castle

Enter GLOUCESTER and BUCKINGHAM, at several doors

GLOUCESTER
How now, my lord, what say the citizens?

BUCKINGHAM
Now, by the holy mother of our Lord,
The citizens are mum and speak not a word.

GLOUCESTER
Touch'd you the bastardy of Edward's children?

BUCKINGHAM
I did; with his contract with Lady Lucy,
And his contract by deputy in France;
The insatiate greediness of his desires,
And his enforcement of the city wives;
His tyranny for trifles; his own bastardy,

As being got, your father then in France,
His resemblance, being not like the duke;
Withal I did infer your lineaments,
Being the right idea of your father,
Both in your form and nobleness of mind;
Laid open all your victories in Scotland,
Your dicipline in war, wisdom in peace,
Your bounty, virtue, fair humility:
Indeed, left nothing fitting for the purpose
Untouch'd, or slightly handled, in discourse
And when mine oratory grew to an end
I bid them that did love their country's good
Cry 'God save Richard, England's royal king!'

GLOUCESTER
Ah! and did they so?

BUCKINGHAM
No, so God help me, they spake not a word;
But, like dumb statues or breathing stones,
Gazed each on other, and look'd deadly pale.
Which when I saw, I reprehended them;
And ask'd the mayor what meant this wilful silence:
His answer was, the people were not wont
To be spoke to but by the recorder.
Then he was urged to tell my tale again,
'Thus saith the duke, thus hath the duke inferr'd;'
But nothing spake in warrant from himself.
When he had done, some followers of mine own,
At the lower end of the hall, hurl'd up their caps,
And some ten voices cried 'God save King Richard!'
And thus I took the vantage of those few,
'Thanks, gentle citizens and friends,' quoth I;
'This general applause and loving shout
Argues your wisdoms and your love to Richard:'
And even here brake off, and came away.

GLOUCESTER
What tongueless blocks were they! would not they speak?

BUCKINGHAM
No, by my troth, my lord.

GLOUCESTER
Will not the mayor then and his brethren come?

BUCKINGHAM
The mayor is here at hand: intend some fear;
Be not you spoke with, but by mighty suit:
And look you get a prayer-book in your hand,
And stand betwixt two churchmen, good my lord;

For on that ground I'll build a holy descant:
And be not easily won to our request:
Play the maid's part, still answer nay, and take it.

GLOUCESTER
I go; and if you plead as well for them
As I can say nay to thee for myself,
No doubt well bring it to a happy issue.

BUCKINGHAM
Go, go, up to the leads; the lord mayor knocks.

Exit GLOUCESTER

Enter the LORD MAYOR and CITIZENS

Welcome my lord; I dance attendance here;
I think the duke will not be spoke withal.

Enter CATESBY

Here comes his servant: how now, Catesby,
What says he?

CATESBY
My lord: he doth entreat your grace;
To visit him to-morrow or next day:
He is within, with two right reverend fathers,
Divinely bent to meditation;
And no worldly suit would he be moved,
To draw him from his holy exercise.

BUCKINGHAM
Return, good Catesby, to thy lord again;
Tell him, myself, the mayor and citizens,
In deep designs and matters of great moment,
No less importing than our general good,
Are come to have some conference with his grace.

CATESBY
I'll tell him what you say, my lord.

Exit

BUCKINGHAM
Ah, ha, my lord, this prince is not an Edward!
He is not lolling on a lewd day-bed,
But on his knees at meditation;
Not dallying with a brace of courtezans,
But meditating with two deep divines;
Not sleeping, to engross his idle body,

But praying, to enrich his watchful soul:
Happy were England, would this gracious prince
Take on himself the sovereignty thereof:
But, sure, I fear, we shall ne'er win him to it.

LORD MAYOR
Marry, God forbid his grace should say us nay!

BUCKINGHAM
I fear he will.

Re-enter CATESBY

How now, Catesby, what says your lord?

CATESBY
My lord,
He wonders to what end you have assembled
Such troops of citizens to speak with him,
His grace not being warn'd thereof before:
My lord, he fears you mean no good to him.

BUCKINGHAM
Sorry I am my noble cousin should
Suspect me, that I mean no good to him:
By heaven, I come in perfect love to him;
And so once more return and tell his grace.

Exit CATESBY

When holy and devout religious men
Are at their beads, 'tis hard to draw them thence,
So sweet is zealous contemplation.

Enter GLOUCESTER aloft, between two Bishops. CATESBY returns

LORD MAYOR
See, where he stands between two clergymen!

BUCKINGHAM
Two props of virtue for a Christian prince,
To stay him from the fall of vanity:
And, see, a book of prayer in his hand,
True ornaments to know a holy man.
Famous Plantagenet, most gracious prince,
Lend favourable ears to our request;
And pardon us the interruption
Of thy devotion and right Christian zeal.

GLOUCESTER

My lord, there needs no such apology:
I rather do beseech you pardon me,
Who, earnest in the service of my God,
Neglect the visitation of my friends.
But, leaving this, what is your grace's pleasure?

BUCKINGHAM
Even that, I hope, which pleaseth God above,
And all good men of this ungovern'd isle.

GLOUCESTER
I do suspect I have done some offence
That seems disgracious in the city's eyes,
And that you come to reprehend my ignorance.

BUCKINGHAM
You have, my lord: would it might please your grace,
At our entreaties, to amend that fault!

GLOUCESTER
Else wherefore breathe I in a Christian land?

BUCKINGHAM
Then know, it is your fault that you resign
The supreme seat, the throne majestical,
The scepter'd office of your ancestors,
Your state of fortune and your due of birth,
The lineal glory of your royal house,
To the corruption of a blemished stock:
Whilst, in the mildness of your sleepy thoughts,
Which here we waken to our country's good,
This noble isle doth want her proper limbs;
Her face defaced with scars of infamy,
Her royal stock graft with ignoble plants,
And almost shoulder'd in the swallowing gulf
Of blind forgetfulness and dark oblivion.
Which to recure, we heartily solicit
Your gracious self to take on you the charge
And kingly government of this your land,
Not as protector, steward, substitute,
Or lowly factor for another's gain;
But as successively from blood to blood,
Your right of birth, your empery, your own.
For this, consorted with the citizens,
Your very worshipful and loving friends,
And by their vehement instigation,
In this just suit come I to move your grace.

GLOUCESTER
I know not whether to depart in silence,
Or bitterly to speak in your reproof.

Best fitteth my degree or your condition
If not to answer, you might haply think
Tongue-tied ambition, not replying, yielded
To bear the golden yoke of sovereignty,
Which fondly you would here impose on me;
If to reprove you for this suit of yours,
So season'd with your faithful love to me.
Then, on the other side, I cheque'd my friends.
Therefore, to speak, and to avoid the first,
And then, in speaking, not to incur the last,
Definitively thus I answer you.
Your love deserves my thanks; but my desert
Unmeritable shuns your high request.
First if all obstacles were cut away,
And that my path were even to the crown,
As my ripe revenue and due by birth
Yet so much is my poverty of spirit,
So mighty and so many my defects,
As I had rather hide me from my greatness,
Being a bark to brook no mighty sea,
Than in my greatness covet to be hid,
And in the vapour of my glory smother'd.
But, God be thank'd, there's no need of me,
And much I need to help you, if need were;
The royal tree hath left us royal fruit,
Which, mellow'd by the stealing hours of time,
Will well become the seat of majesty,
And make, no doubt, us happy by his reign.
On him I lay what you would lay on me,
The right and fortune of his happy stars;
Which God defend that I should wring from him!

BUCKINGHAM
My lord, this argues conscience in your grace;
But the respects thereof are nice and trivial,
All circumstances well considered.
You say that Edward is your brother's son:
So say we too, but not by Edward's wife;
For first he was contract to Lady Lucy—
Your mother lives a witness to that vow—
And afterward by substitute betroth'd
To Bona, sister to the King of France.
These both put by a poor petitioner,
A care-crazed mother of a many children,
A beauty-waning and distressed widow,
Even in the afternoon of her best days,
Made prize and purchase of his lustful eye,
Seduced the pitch and height of all his thoughts
To base declension and loathed bigamy
By her, in his unlawful bed, he got
This Edward, whom our manners term the prince.

More bitterly could I expostulate,
Save that, for reverence to some alive,
I give a sparing limit to my tongue.
Then, good my lord, take to your royal self
This proffer'd benefit of dignity;
If non to bless us and the land withal,
Yet to draw forth your noble ancestry
From the corruption of abusing times,
Unto a lineal true-derived course.

LORD MAYOR
Do, good my lord, your citizens entreat you.

BUCKINGHAM
Refuse not, mighty lord, this proffer'd love.

CATESBY
O, make them joyful, grant their lawful suit!

GLOUCESTER
Alas, why would you heap these cares on me?
I am unfit for state and majesty;
I do beseech you, take it not amiss;
I cannot nor I will not yield to you.

BUCKINGHAM
If you refuse it,—as, in love and zeal,
Loath to depose the child, Your brother's son;
As well we know your tenderness of heart
And gentle, kind, effeminate remorse,
Which we have noted in you to your kin,
And egally indeed to all estates,—
Yet whether you accept our suit or no,
Your brother's son shall never reign our king;
But we will plant some other in the throne,
To the disgrace and downfall of your house:
And in this resolution here we leave you.—
Come, citizens: 'zounds! I'll entreat no more.

GLOUCESTER
O, do not swear, my lord of Buckingham.

Exit BUCKINGHAM with the CITIZENS

CATESBY
Call them again, my lord, and accept their suit.

ANOTHER
Do, good my lord, lest all the land do rue it.

GLOUCESTER

Would you enforce me to a world of care?
Well, call them again. I am not made of stone,
But penetrable to your. kind entreats,
Albeit against my conscience and my soul.

Re-enter BUCKINGHAM and the rest

Cousin of Buckingham, and you sage, grave men,
Since you will buckle fortune on my back,
To bear her burthen, whether I will or no,
I must have patience to endure the load:
But if black scandal or foul-faced reproach
Attend the sequel of your imposition,
Your mere enforcement shall acquittance me
From all the impure blots and stains thereof;
For God he knows, and you may partly see,
How far I am from the desire thereof.

LORD AMYOR
God bless your grace! we see it, and will say it.

GLOUCESTER
In saying so, you shall but say the truth.

BUCKINGHAM
Then I salute you with this kingly title:
Long live Richard, England's royal king!

Lord Mayor Citizens
Amen.

BUCKINGHAM
To-morrow will it please you to be crown'd?

GLOUCESTER
Even when you please, since you will have it so.

BUCKINGHAM
To-morrow, then, we will attend your grace:
And so most joyfully we take our leave.

GLOUCESTER
Come, let us to our holy task again.
Farewell, good cousin; farewell, gentle friends.

Exeunt

SCENE I. Before the Tower

Enter, on one side, QUEEN ELIZABETH, DUCHESS OF YORK, and DORSET; on the other, ANNE, Duchess of Gloucester, leading Lady Margaret Plantagenet, CLARENCE's young Daughter

DUCHESS OF YORK
Who meets us here? my niece Plantagenet
Led in the hand of her kind aunt of Gloucester?
Now, for my life, she's wandering to the Tower,
On pure heart's love to greet the tender princes.
Daughter, well met.

LADY ANNE
God give your graces both
A happy and a joyful time of day!

QUEEN ELIZABETH
As much to you, good sister! Whither away?

LADY ANNE
No farther than the Tower; and, as I guess,
Upon the like devotion as yourselves,
To gratulate the gentle princes there.

QUEEN ELIZABETH
Kind sister, thanks: we'll enter all together.

Enter BRAKENBURY

And, in good time, here the lieutenant comes.
Master lieutenant, pray you, by your leave,
How doth the prince, and my young son of York?

BRAKENBURY
Right well, dear madam. By your patience,
I may not suffer you to visit them;
The king hath straitly charged the contrary.

QUEEN ELIZABETH
The king! why, who's that?

BRAKENBURY
I cry you mercy: I mean the lord protector.

QUEEN ELIZABETH
The Lord protect him from that kingly title!
Hath he set bounds betwixt their love and me?
I am their mother; who should keep me from them?

DUCHESS OF YORK

I am their fathers mother; I will see them.

LADY ANNE
Their aunt I am in law, in love their mother:
Then bring me to their sights; I'll bear thy blame
And take thy office from thee, on my peril.

BRAKENBURY
No, madam, no; I may not leave it so:
I am bound by oath, and therefore pardon me.

Exit

Enter LORD STANLEY

LORD STANLEY
Let me but meet you, ladies, one hour hence,
And I'll salute your grace of York as mother,
And reverend looker on, of two fair queens.

To LADY ANNE

Come, madam, you must straight to Westminster,
There to be crowned Richard's royal queen.

QUEEN ELIZABETH
O, cut my lace in sunder, that my pent heart
May have some scope to beat, or else I swoon
With this dead-killing news!

LADY ANNE
Despiteful tidings! O unpleasing news!

DORSET
Be of good cheer: mother, how fares your grace?

QUEEN ELIZABETH
O Dorset, speak not to me, get thee hence!
Death and destruction dog thee at the heels;
Thy mother's name is ominous to children.
If thou wilt outstrip death, go cross the seas,
And live with Richmond, from the reach of hell
Go, hie thee, hie thee from this slaughter-house,
Lest thou increase the number of the dead;
And make me die the thrall of Margaret's curse,
Nor mother, wife, nor England's counted queen.

LORD STANLEY
Full of wise care is this your counsel, madam.
Take all the swift advantage of the hours;
You shall have letters from me to my son

To meet you on the way, and welcome you.
Be not ta'en tardy by unwise delay.

DUCHESS OF YORK
O ill-dispersing wind of misery!
O my accursed womb, the bed of death!
A cockatrice hast thou hatch'd to the world,
Whose unavoided eye is murderous.

LORD STANLEY
Come, madam, come; I in all haste was sent.

LADY ANNE
And I in all unwillingness will go.
I would to God that the inclusive verge
Of golden metal that must round my brow
Were red-hot steel, to sear me to the brain!
Anointed let me be with deadly venom,
And die, ere men can say, God save the queen!

QUEEN ELIZABETH
Go, go, poor soul, I envy not thy glory
To feed my humour, wish thyself no harm.

LADY ANNE
No! why? When he that is my husband now
Came to me, as I follow'd Henry's corse,
When scarce the blood was well wash'd from his hands
Which issued from my other angel husband
And that dead saint which then I weeping follow'd;
O, when, I say, I look'd on Richard's face,
This was my wish: 'Be thou,' quoth I, ' accursed,
For making me, so young, so old a widow!
And, when thou wed'st, let sorrow haunt thy bed;
And be thy wife—if any be so mad—
As miserable by the life of thee
As thou hast made me by my dear lord's death!
Lo, ere I can repeat this curse again,
Even in so short a space, my woman's heart
Grossly grew captive to his honey words
And proved the subject of my own soul's curse,
Which ever since hath kept my eyes from rest;
For never yet one hour in his bed
Have I enjoy'd the golden dew of sleep,
But have been waked by his timorous dreams.
Besides, he hates me for my father Warwick;
And will, no doubt, shortly be rid of me.

QUEEN ELIZABETH
Poor heart, adieu! I pity thy complaining.

LADY ANNE
No more than from my soul I mourn for yours.

QUEEN ELIZABETH
Farewell, thou woful welcomer of glory!

LADY ANNE
Adieu, poor soul, that takest thy leave of it!

DUCHESS OF YORK
[To **DORSET**]
Go thou to Richmond, and good fortune guide thee!

To **LADY ANNE**
Go thou to Richard, and good angels guard thee!

To **QUEEN ELIZABETH**
Go thou to sanctuary, and good thoughts possess thee!
I to my grave, where peace and rest lie with me!
Eighty odd years of sorrow have I seen,
And each hour's joy wrecked with a week of teen.

QUEEN ELIZABETH
Stay, yet look back with me unto the Tower.
Pity, you ancient stones, those tender babes
Whom envy hath immured within your walls!
Rough cradle for such little pretty ones!
Rude ragged nurse, old sullen playfellow
For tender princes, use my babies well!
So foolish sorrow bids your stones farewell.

Exeunt

SCENE II. London. The Palace

Sennet.

Enter KING RICHARD III, in pomp, crowned; BUCKINGHAM, CATESBY, a page, and others

KING RICHARD III
Stand all apart Cousin of Buckingham!

BUCKINGHAM
My gracious sovereign?

KING RICHARD III
Give me thy hand.

Here he ascendeth his throne

Thus high, by thy advice
And thy assistance, is King Richard seated;
But shall we wear these honours for a day?
Or shall they last, and we rejoice in them?

BUCKINGHAM
Still live they and for ever may they last!

KING RICHARD III
O Buckingham, now do I play the touch,
To try if thou be current gold indeed
Young Edward lives: think now what I would say.

BUCKINGHAM
Say on, my loving lord.

KING RICHARD III
Why, Buckingham, I say, I would be king,

BUCKINGHAM
Why, so you are, my thrice renowned liege.

KING RICHARD III
Ha! am I king? 'tis so: but Edward lives.

BUCKINGHAM
True, noble prince.

KING RICHARD III
O bitter consequence,
That Edward still should live! 'True, noble prince!'
Cousin, thou wert not wont to be so dull:
Shall I be plain? I wish the bastards dead;
And I would have it suddenly perform'd.
What sayest thou? speak suddenly; be brief.

BUCKINGHAM
Your grace may do your pleasure.

KING RICHARD III
Tut, tut, thou art all ice, thy kindness freezeth:
Say, have I thy consent that they shall die?

BUCKINGHAM
Give me some breath, some little pause, my lord
Before I positively herein:
I will resolve your grace immediately.

Exit

CATESBY
[Aside to a stander by]
The king is angry: see, he bites the lip.

KING RICHARD III
I will converse with iron-witted fools
And unrespective boys: none are for me
That look into me with considerate eyes:
High-reaching Buckingham grows circumspect.
Boy!

PAGE
My lord?

KING RICHARD III
Know'st thou not any whom corrupting gold
Would tempt unto a close exploit of death?

PAGE
My lord, I know a discontented gentleman,
Whose humble means match not his haughty mind:
Gold were as good as twenty orators,
And will, no doubt, tempt him to any thing.

KING RICHARD III
What is his name?

PAGE
His name, my lord, is Tyrrel.

KING RICHARD III
I partly know the man: go, call him hither.

Exit PAGE

The deep-revolving witty Buckingham
No more shall be the neighbour to my counsel:
Hath he so long held out with me untired,
And stops he now for breath?

Enter STANLEY

How now! what news with you?

STANLEY
My lord, I hear the Marquis Dorset's fled
To Richmond, in those parts beyond the sea
Where he abides.

Stands apart

KING RICHARD III
Catesby!

CATESBY
My lord?

KING RICHARD III
Rumour it abroad
That Anne, my wife, is sick and like to die:
I will take order for her keeping close.
Inquire me out some mean-born gentleman,
Whom I will marry straight to Clarence' daughter:
The boy is foolish, and I fear not him.
Look, how thou dream'st! I say again, give out
That Anne my wife is sick and like to die:
About it; for it stands me much upon,
To stop all hopes whose growth may damage me.

Exit CATESBY

I must be married to my brother's daughter,
Or else my kingdom stands on brittle glass.
Murder her brothers, and then marry her!
Uncertain way of gain! But I am in
So far in blood that sin will pluck on sin:
Tear-falling pity dwells not in this eye.

Re-enter PAGE, with TYRREL

Is thy name Tyrrel?

TYRREL
James Tyrrel, and your most obedient subject.

KING RICHARD III
Art thou, indeed?

TYRREL
Prove me, my gracious sovereign.

KING RICHARD III
Darest thou resolve to kill a friend of mine?

TYRREL
Ay, my lord;
But I had rather kill two enemies.

KING RICHARD III
Why, there thou hast it: two deep enemies,
Foes to my rest and my sweet sleep's disturbers

Are they that I would have thee deal upon:
Tyrrel, I mean those bastards in the Tower.

TYRREL
Let me have open means to come to them,
And soon I'll rid you from the fear of them.

KING RICHARD III
Thou sing'st sweet music. Hark, come hither, Tyrrel
Go, by this token: rise, and lend thine ear:

Whispers

There is no more but so: say it is done,
And I will love thee, and prefer thee too.

TYRREL
'Tis done, my gracious lord.

KING RICHARD III
Shall we hear from thee, Tyrrel, ere we sleep?

TYRREL
Ye shall, my Lord.

Exit

Re-enter BUCKINGHAM

BUCKINGHAM
My Lord, I have consider'd in my mind
The late demand that you did sound me in.

KING RICHARD III
Well, let that pass. Dorset is fled to Richmond.

BUCKINGHAM
I hear that news, my lord.

KING RICHARD III
Stanley, he is your wife's son well, look to it.

BUCKINGHAM
My lord, I claim your gift, my due by promise,
For which your honour and your faith is pawn'd;
The earldom of Hereford and the moveables
The which you promised I should possess.

KING RICHARD III
Stanley, look to your wife; if she convey
Letters to Richmond, you shall answer it.

BUCKINGHAM
What says your highness to my just demand?

KING RICHARD III
As I remember, Henry the Sixth
Did prophesy that Richmond should be king,
When Richmond was a little peevish boy.
A king, perhaps, perhaps,—

BUCKINGHAM
My lord!

KING RICHARD III
How chance the prophet could not at that time
Have told me, I being by, that I should kill him?

BUCKINGHAM
My lord, your promise for the earldom,—

KING RICHARD III
Richmond! When last I was at Exeter,
The mayor in courtesy show'd me the castle,
And call'd it Rougemont: at which name I started,
Because a bard of Ireland told me once
I should not live long after I saw Richmond.

BUCKINGHAM
My Lord!

KING RICHARD III
Ay, what's o'clock?

BUCKINGHAM
I am thus bold to put your grace in mind
Of what you promised me.

KING RICHARD III
Well, but what's o'clock?

BUCKINGHAM
Upon the stroke of ten.

KING RICHARD III
Well, let it strike.

BUCKINGHAM
Why let it strike?

KING RICHARD III

Because that, like a Jack, thou keep'st the stroke
Betwixt thy begging and my meditation.
I am not in the giving vein to-day.

BUCKINGHAM
Why, then resolve me whether you will or no.

KING RICHARD III
Tut, tut,
Thou troublest me; am not in the vein.

Exeunt all but BUCKINGHAM

BUCKINGHAM
Is it even so? rewards he my true service
With such deep contempt made I him king for this?
O, let me think on Hastings, and be gone
To Brecknock, while my fearful head is on!

Exit

SCENE III. The Same

Enter TYRREL

TYRREL
The tyrannous and bloody deed is done.
The most arch of piteous massacre
That ever yet this land was guilty of.
Dighton and Forrest, whom I did suborn
To do this ruthless piece of butchery,
Although they were flesh'd villains, bloody dogs,
Melting with tenderness and kind compassion
Wept like two children in their deaths' sad stories.
'Lo, thus' quoth Dighton, 'lay those tender babes:'
'Thus, thus,' quoth Forrest, 'girdling one another
Within their innocent alabaster arms:
Their lips were four red roses on a stalk,
Which in their summer beauty kiss'd each other.
A book of prayers on their pillow lay;
Which once,' quoth Forrest, 'almost changed my mind;
But O! the devil'—there the villain stopp'd
Whilst Dighton thus told on: 'We smothered
The most replenished sweet work of nature,
That from the prime creation e'er she framed.'
Thus both are gone with conscience and remorse;
They could not speak; and so I left them both,
To bring this tidings to the bloody king.
And here he comes.

Enter KING RICHARD III

All hail, my sovereign liege!

KING RICHARD III
Kind Tyrrel, am I happy in thy news?

TYRREL
If to have done the thing you gave in charge
Beget your happiness, be happy then,
For it is done, my lord.

KING RICHARD III
But didst thou see them dead?

TYRREL
I did, my lord.

KING RICHARD III
And buried, gentle Tyrrel?

TYRREL
The chaplain of the Tower hath buried them;
But how or in what place I do not know.

KING RICHARD III
Come to me, Tyrrel, soon at after supper,
And thou shalt tell the process of their death.
Meantime, but think how I may do thee good,
And be inheritor of thy desire.
Farewell till soon.

Exit TYRREL

The son of Clarence have I pent up close;
His daughter meanly have I match'd in marriage;
The sons of Edward sleep in Abraham's bosom,
And Anne my wife hath bid the world good night.
Now, for I know the Breton Richmond aims
At young Elizabeth, my brother's daughter,
And, by that knot, looks proudly o'er the crown,
To her I go, a jolly thriving wooer.

Enter CATESBY

CATESBY
My lord!

KING RICHARD III
Good news or bad, that thou comest in so bluntly?

CATESBY
Bad news, my lord: Ely is fled to Richmond;
And Buckingham, back'd with the hardy Welshmen,
Is in the field, and still his power increaseth.

KING RICHARD III
Ely with Richmond troubles me more near
Than Buckingham and his rash-levied army.
Come, I have heard that fearful commenting
Is leaden servitor to dull delay;
Delay leads impotent and snail-paced beggary
Then fiery expedition be my wing,
Jove's Mercury, and herald for a king!
Come, muster men: my counsel is my shield;
We must be brief when traitors brave the field.

Exeunt

SCENE IV. Before The Palace

Enter QUEEN MARGARET

QUEEN MARGARET
So, now prosperity begins to mellow
And drop into the rotten mouth of death.
Here in these confines slily have I lurk'd,
To watch the waning of mine adversaries.
A dire induction am I witness to,
And will to France, hoping the consequence
Will prove as bitter, black, and tragical.
Withdraw thee, wretched Margaret: who comes here?

Enter QUEEN ELIZABETH and the DUCHESS OF YORK

QUEEN ELIZABETH
Ah, my young princes! ah, my tender babes!
My unblown flowers, new-appearing sweets!
If yet your gentle souls fly in the air
And be not fix'd in doom perpetual,
Hover about me with your airy wings
And hear your mother's lamentation!

QUEEN MARGARET
Hover about her; say, that right for right
Hath dimm'd your infant morn to aged night.

DUCHESS OF YORK

So many miseries have crazed my voice,
That my woe-wearied tongue is mute and dumb,
Edward Plantagenet, why art thou dead?

QUEEN MARGARET
Plantagenet doth quit Plantagenet.
Edward for Edward pays a dying debt.

QUEEN ELIZABETH
Wilt thou, O God, fly from such gentle lambs,
And throw them in the entrails of the wolf?
When didst thou sleep when such a deed was done?

QUEEN MARGARET
When holy Harry died, and my sweet son.

DUCHESS OF YORK
Blind sight, dead life, poor mortal living ghost,
Woe's scene, world's shame, grave's due by life usurp'd,
Brief abstract and record of tedious days,
Rest thy unrest on England's lawful earth,

Sitting down

Unlawfully made drunk with innocents' blood!

QUEEN ELIZABETH
O, that thou wouldst as well afford a grave
As thou canst yield a melancholy seat!
Then would I hide my bones, not rest them here.
O, who hath any cause to mourn but I?

Sitting down by her

QUEEN MARGARET
If ancient sorrow be most reverend,
Give mine the benefit of seniory,
And let my woes frown on the upper hand.
If sorrow can admit society,

Sitting down with them

Tell o'er your woes again by viewing mine:
I had an Edward, till a Richard kill'd him;
I had a Harry, till a Richard kill'd him:
Thou hadst an Edward, till a Richard kill'd him;
Thou hadst a Richard, till a Richard killed him;

DUCHESS OF YORK
I had a Richard too, and thou didst kill him;
I had a Rutland too, thou holp'st to kill him.

QUEEN MARGARET
Thou hadst a Clarence too, and Richard kill'd him.
From forth the kennel of thy womb hath crept
A hell-hound that doth hunt us all to death:
That dog, that had his teeth before his eyes,
To worry lambs and lap their gentle blood,
That foul defacer of God's handiwork,
That excellent grand tyrant of the earth,
That reigns in galled eyes of weeping souls,
Thy womb let loose, to chase us to our graves.
O upright, just, and true-disposing God,
How do I thank thee, that this carnal cur
Preys on the issue of his mother's body,
And makes her pew-fellow with others' moan!

DUCHESS OF YORK
O Harry's wife, triumph not in my woes!
God witness with me, I have wept for thine.

QUEEN MARGARET
Bear with me; I am hungry for revenge,
And now I cloy me with beholding it.
Thy Edward he is dead, that stabb'd my Edward:
Thy other Edward dead, to quit my Edward;
Young York he is but boot, because both they
Match not the high perfection of my loss:
Thy Clarence he is dead that kill'd my Edward;
And the beholders of this tragic play,
The adulterate Hastings, Rivers, Vaughan, Grey,
Untimely smother'd in their dusky graves.
Richard yet lives, hell's black intelligencer,
Only reserved their factor, to buy souls
And send them thither: but at hand, at hand,
Ensues his piteous and unpitied end:
Earth gapes, hell burns, fiends roar, saints pray.
To have him suddenly convey'd away.
Cancel his bond of life, dear God, I prey,
That I may live to say, The dog is dead!

QUEEN ELIZABETH
O, thou didst prophesy the time would come
That I should wish for thee to help me curse
That bottled spider, that foul bunch-back'd toad!

QUEEN MARGARET
I call'd thee then vain flourish of my fortune;
I call'd thee then poor shadow, painted queen;
The presentation of but what I was;
The flattering index of a direful pageant;
One heaved a-high, to be hurl'd down below;

A mother only mock'd with two sweet babes;
A dream of what thou wert, a breath, a bubble,
A sign of dignity, a garish flag,
To be the aim of every dangerous shot,
A queen in jest, only to fill the scene.
Where is thy husband now? where be thy brothers?
Where are thy children? wherein dost thou, joy?
Who sues to thee and cries 'God save the queen'?
Where be the bending peers that flatter'd thee?
Where be the thronging troops that follow'd thee?
Decline all this, and see what now thou art:
For happy wife, a most distressed widow;
For joyful mother, one that wails the name;
For queen, a very caitiff crown'd with care;
For one being sued to, one that humbly sues;
For one that scorn'd at me, now scorn'd of me;
For one being fear'd of all, now fearing one;
For one commanding all, obey'd of none.
Thus hath the course of justice wheel'd about,
And left thee but a very prey to time;
Having no more but thought of what thou wert,
To torture thee the more, being what thou art.
Thou didst usurp my place, and dost thou not
Usurp the just proportion of my sorrow?
Now thy proud neck bears half my burthen'd yoke;
From which even here I slip my weary neck,
And leave the burthen of it all on thee.
Farewell, York's wife, and queen of sad mischance:
These English woes will make me smile in France.

QUEEN ELIZABETH
O thou well skill'd in curses, stay awhile,
And teach me how to curse mine enemies!

QUEEN MARGARET
Forbear to sleep the nights, and fast the days;
Compare dead happiness with living woe;
Think that thy babes were fairer than they were,
And he that slew them fouler than he is:
Bettering thy loss makes the bad causer worse:
Revolving this will teach thee how to curse.

QUEEN ELIZABETH
My words are dull; O, quicken them with thine!

QUEEN MARGARET
Thy woes will make them sharp, and pierce like mine.

Exit

DUCHESS OF YORK

Why should calamity be full of words?

QUEEN ELIZABETH
Windy attorneys to their client woes,
Airy succeeders of intestate joys,
Poor breathing orators of miseries!
Let them have scope: though what they do impart
Help not all, yet do they ease the heart.

DUCHESS OF YORK
If so, then be not tongue-tied: go with me.
And in the breath of bitter words let's smother
My damned son, which thy two sweet sons smother'd.
I hear his drum: be copious in exclaims.

Enter KING RICHARD III, marching, with drums and trumpets

KING RICHARD III
Who intercepts my expedition?

DUCHESS OF YORK
O, she that might have intercepted thee,
By strangling thee in her accursed womb
From all the slaughters, wretch, that thou hast done!

QUEEN ELIZABETH
Hidest thou that forehead with a golden crown,
Where should be graven, if that right were right,
The slaughter of the prince that owed that crown,
And the dire death of my two sons and brothers?
Tell me, thou villain slave, where are my children?

DUCHESS OF YORK
Thou toad, thou toad, where is thy brother Clarence?
And little Ned Plantagenet, his son?

QUEEN ELIZABETH
Where is kind Hastings, Rivers, Vaughan, Grey?

KING RICHARD III
A flourish, trumpets! strike alarum, drums!
Let not the heavens hear these tell-tale women
Rail on the Lord's enointed: strike, I say!

Flourish. Alarums

Either be patient, and entreat me fair,
Or with the clamorous report of war
Thus will I drown your exclamations.

DUCHESS OF YORK

Art thou my son?

KING RICHARD III
Ay, I thank God, my father, and yourself.

DUCHESS OF YORK
Then patiently hear my impatience.

KING RICHARD III
Madam, I have a touch of your condition,
Which cannot brook the accent of reproof.

DUCHESS OF YORK
O, let me speak!

KING RICHARD III
Do then: but I'll not hear.

DUCHESS OF YORK
I will be mild and gentle in my speech.

KING RICHARD III
And brief, good mother; for I am in haste.

DUCHESS OF YORK
Art thou so hasty? I have stay'd for thee,
God knows, in anguish, pain and agony.

KING RICHARD III
And came I not at last to comfort you?

DUCHESS OF YORK
No, by the holy rood, thou know'st it well,
Thou camest on earth to make the earth my hell.
A grievous burthen was thy birth to me;
Tetchy and wayward was thy infancy;
Thy school-days frightful, desperate, wild, and furious,
Thy prime of manhood daring, bold, and venturous,
Thy age confirm'd, proud, subdued, bloody, treacherous,
More mild, but yet more harmful, kind in hatred:
What comfortable hour canst thou name,
That ever graced me in thy company?

KING RICHARD III
Faith, none, but Humphrey Hour, that call'd your grace
To breakfast once forth of my company.
If I be so disgracious in your sight,
Let me march on, and not offend your grace.
Strike the drum.

DUCHESS OF YORK

I prithee, hear me speak.

KING RICHARD III
You speak too bitterly.

DUCHESS OF YORK
Hear me a word;
For I shall never speak to thee again.

KING RICHARD III
So.

DUCHESS OF YORK
Either thou wilt die, by God's just ordinance,
Ere from this war thou turn a conqueror,
Or I with grief and extreme age shall perish
And never look upon thy face again.
Therefore take with thee my most heavy curse;
Which, in the day of battle, tire thee more
Than all the complete armour that thou wear'st!
My prayers on the adverse party fight;
And there the little souls of Edward's children
Whisper the spirits of thine enemies
And promise them success and victory.
Bloody thou art, bloody will be thy end;
Shame serves thy life and doth thy death attend.

Exit

QUEEN ELIZABETH
Though far more cause, yet much less spirit to curse
Abides in me; I say amen to all.

KING RICHARD III
Stay, madam; I must speak a word with you.

QUEEN ELIZABETH
I have no more sons of the royal blood
For thee to murder: for my daughters, Richard,
They shall be praying nuns, not weeping queens;
And therefore level not to hit their lives.

KING RICHARD III
You have a daughter call'd Elizabeth,
Virtuous and fair, royal and gracious.

QUEEN ELIZABETH
And must she die for this? O, let her live,
And I'll corrupt her manners, stain her beauty;
Slander myself as false to Edward's bed;
Throw over her the veil of infamy:

So she may live unscarr'd of bleeding slaughter,
I will confess she was not Edward's daughter.

KING RICHARD III
Wrong not her birth, she is of royal blood.

QUEEN ELIZABETH
To save her life, I'll say she is not so.

KING RICHARD III
Her life is only safest in her birth.

QUEEN ELIZABETH
And only in that safety died her brothers.

KING RICHARD III
Lo, at their births good stars were opposite.

QUEEN ELIZABETH
No, to their lives bad friends were contrary.

KING RICHARD III
All unavoided is the doom of destiny.

QUEEN ELIZABETH
True, when avoided grace makes destiny:
My babes were destined to a fairer death,
If grace had bless'd thee with a fairer life.

KING RICHARD III
You speak as if that I had slain my cousins.

QUEEN ELIZABETH
Cousins, indeed; and by their uncle cozen'd
Of comfort, kingdom, kindred, freedom, life.
Whose hand soever lanced their tender hearts,
Thy head, all indirectly, gave direction:
No doubt the murderous knife was dull and blunt
Till it was whetted on thy stone-hard heart,
To revel in the entrails of my lambs.
But that still use of grief makes wild grief tame,
My tongue should to thy ears not name my boys
Till that my nails were anchor'd in thine eyes;
And I, in such a desperate bay of death,
Like a poor bark, of sails and tackling reft,
Rush all to pieces on thy rocky bosom.

KING RICHARD III
Madam, so thrive I in my enterprise
And dangerous success of bloody wars,

As I intend more good to you and yours,
Than ever you or yours were by me wrong'd!

QUEEN ELIZABETH
What good is cover'd with the face of heaven,
To be discover'd, that can do me good?

KING RICHARD III
The advancement of your children, gentle lady.

QUEEN ELIZABETH
Up to some scaffold, there to lose their heads?

KING RICHARD III
No, to the dignity and height of honour
The high imperial type of this earth's glory.

QUEEN ELIZABETH
Flatter my sorrows with report of it;
Tell me what state, what dignity, what honour,
Canst thou demise to any child of mine?

KING RICHARD III
Even all I have; yea, and myself and all,
Will I withal endow a child of thine;
So in the Lethe of thy angry soul
Thou drown the sad remembrance of those wrongs
Which thou supposest I have done to thee.

QUEEN ELIZABETH
Be brief, lest that be process of thy kindness
Last longer telling than thy kindness' date.

KING RICHARD III
Then know, that from my soul I love thy daughter.

QUEEN ELIZABETH
My daughter's mother thinks it with her soul.

KING RICHARD III
What do you think?

QUEEN ELIZABETH
That thou dost love my daughter from thy soul:
So from thy soul's love didst thou love her brothers;
And from my heart's love I do thank thee for it.

KING RICHARD III
Be not so hasty to confound my meaning:
I mean, that with my soul I love thy daughter,
And mean to make her queen of England.

QUEEN ELIZABETH
Say then, who dost thou mean shall be her king?

KING RICHARD III
Even he that makes her queen who should be else?

QUEEN ELIZABETH
What, thou?

KING RICHARD III
I, even I: what think you of it, madam?

QUEEN ELIZABETH
How canst thou woo her?

KING RICHARD III
That would I learn of you,
As one that are best acquainted with her humour.

QUEEN ELIZABETH
And wilt thou learn of me?

KING RICHARD III
Madam, with all my heart.

QUEEN ELIZABETH
Send to her, by the man that slew her brothers,
A pair of bleeding-hearts; thereon engrave
Edward and York; then haply she will weep:
Therefore present to her—as sometime Margaret
Did to thy father, steep'd in Rutland's blood,—
A handkerchief; which, say to her, did drain
The purple sap from her sweet brother's body
And bid her dry her weeping eyes therewith.
If this inducement force her not to love,
Send her a story of thy noble acts;
Tell her thou madest away her uncle Clarence,
Her uncle Rivers; yea, and, for her sake,
Madest quick conveyance with her good aunt Anne.

KING RICHARD III
Come, come, you mock me; this is not the way
To win our daughter.

QUEEN ELIZABETH
There is no other way
Unless thou couldst put on some other shape,
And not be Richard that hath done all this.

KING RICHARD III

Say that I did all this for love of her.

QUEEN ELIZABETH
Nay, then indeed she cannot choose but hate thee,
Having bought love with such a bloody spoil.

KING RICHARD III
Look, what is done cannot be now amended:
Men shall deal unadvisedly sometimes,
Which after hours give leisure to repent.
If I did take the kingdom from your sons,
To make amends, Ill give it to your daughter.
If I have kill'd the issue of your womb,
To quicken your increase, I will beget
Mine issue of your blood upon your daughter
A grandam's name is little less in love
Than is the doting title of a mother;
They are as children but one step below,
Even of your mettle, of your very blood;
Of an one pain, save for a night of groans
Endured of her, for whom you bid like sorrow.
Your children were vexation to your youth,
But mine shall be a comfort to your age.
The loss you have is but a son being king,
And by that loss your daughter is made queen.
I cannot make you what amends I would,
Therefore accept such kindness as I can.
Dorset your son, that with a fearful soul
Leads discontented steps in foreign soil,
This fair alliance quickly shall call home
To high promotions and great dignity:
The king, that calls your beauteous daughter wife.
Familiarly shall call thy Dorset brother;
Again shall you be mother to a king,
And all the ruins of distressful times
Repair'd with double riches of content.
What! we have many goodly days to see:
The liquid drops of tears that you have shed
Shall come again, transform'd to orient pearl,
Advantaging their loan with interest
Of ten times double gain of happiness.
Go, then my mother, to thy daughter go
Make bold her bashful years with your experience;
Prepare her ears to hear a wooer's tale
Put in her tender heart the aspiring flame
Of golden sovereignty; acquaint the princess
With the sweet silent hours of marriage joys
And when this arm of mine hath chastised
The petty rebel, dull-brain'd Buckingham,
Bound with triumphant garlands will I come
And lead thy daughter to a conqueror's bed;

To whom I will retail my conquest won,
And she shall be sole victress, Caesar's Caesar.

QUEEN ELIZABETH
What were I best to say? her father's brother
Would be her lord? or shall I say, her uncle?
Or, he that slew her brothers and her uncles?
Under what title shall I woo for thee,
That God, the law, my honour and her love,
Can make seem pleasing to her tender years?

KING RICHARD III
Infer fair England's peace by this alliance.

QUEEN ELIZABETH
Which she shall purchase with still lasting war.

KING RICHARD III
Say that the king, which may command, entreats.

QUEEN ELIZABETH
That at her hands which the king's King forbids.

KING RICHARD III
Say, she shall be a high and mighty queen.

QUEEN ELIZABETH
To wail the tide, as her mother doth.

KING RICHARD III
Say, I will love her everlastingly.

QUEEN ELIZABETH
But how long shall that title 'ever' last?

KING RICHARD III
Sweetly in force unto her fair life's end.

QUEEN ELIZABETH
But how long fairly shall her sweet lie last?

KING RICHARD III
So long as heaven and nature lengthens it.

QUEEN ELIZABETH
So long as hell and Richard likes of it.

KING RICHARD III
Say, I, her sovereign, am her subject love.

QUEEN ELIZABETH

But she, your subject, loathes such sovereignty.

KING RICHARD III
Be eloquent in my behalf to her.

QUEEN ELIZABETH
An honest tale speeds best being plainly told.

KING RICHARD III
Then in plain terms tell her my loving tale.

QUEEN ELIZABETH
Plain and not honest is too harsh a style.

KING RICHARD III
Your reasons are too shallow and too quick.

QUEEN ELIZABETH
O no, my reasons are too deep and dead;
Too deep and dead, poor infants, in their grave.

KING RICHARD III
Harp not on that string, madam; that is past.

QUEEN ELIZABETH
Harp on it still shall I till heart-strings break.

KING RICHARD III
Now, by my George, my garter, and my crown,—

QUEEN ELIZABETH
Profaned, dishonour'd, and the third usurp'd.

KING RICHARD III
I swear—

QUEEN ELIZABETH
By nothing; for this is no oath:
The George, profaned, hath lost his holy honour;
The garter, blemish'd, pawn'd his knightly virtue;
The crown, usurp'd, disgraced his kingly glory.
if something thou wilt swear to be believed,
Swear then by something that thou hast not wrong'd.

KING RICHARD III
Now, by the world—

QUEEN ELIZABETH
'Tis full of thy foul wrongs.

KING RICHARD III

My father's death—

QUEEN ELIZABETH
Thy life hath that dishonour'd.

KING RICHARD III
Then, by myself—

QUEEN ELIZABETH
Thyself thyself misusest.

KING RICHARD III
Why then, by God—

QUEEN ELIZABETH
God's wrong is most of all.
If thou hadst fear'd to break an oath by Him,
The unity the king thy brother made
Had not been broken, nor my brother slain:
If thou hadst fear'd to break an oath by Him,
The imperial metal, circling now thy brow,
Had graced the tender temples of my child,
And both the princes had been breathing here,
Which now, two tender playfellows to dust,
Thy broken faith hath made a prey for worms.
What canst thou swear by now?

KING RICHARD III
The time to come.

QUEEN ELIZABETH
That thou hast wronged in the time o'erpast;
For I myself have many tears to wash
Hereafter time, for time past wrong'd by thee.
The children live, whose parents thou hast slaughter'd,
Ungovern'd youth, to wail it in their age;
The parents live, whose children thou hast butcher'd,
Old wither'd plants, to wail it with their age.
Swear not by time to come; for that thou hast
Misused ere used, by time misused o'erpast.

KING RICHARD III
As I intend to prosper and repent,
So thrive I in my dangerous attempt
Of hostile arms! myself myself confound!
Heaven and fortune bar me happy hours!
Day, yield me not thy light; nor, night, thy rest!
Be opposite all planets of good luck
To my proceedings, if, with pure heart's love,
Immaculate devotion, holy thoughts,
I tender not thy beauteous princely daughter!

In her consists my happiness and thine;
Without her, follows to this land and me,
To thee, herself, and many a Christian soul,
Death, desolation, ruin and decay:
It cannot be avoided but by this;
It will not be avoided but by this.
Therefore, good mother,—I must can you so—
Be the attorney of my love to her:
Plead what I will be, not what I have been;
Not my deserts, but what I will deserve:
Urge the necessity and state of times,
And be not peevish-fond in great designs.

QUEEN ELIZABETH
Shall I be tempted of the devil thus?

KING RICHARD III
Ay, if the devil tempt thee to do good.

QUEEN ELIZABETH
Shall I forget myself to be myself?

KING RICHARD III
Ay, if yourself's remembrance wrong yourself.

QUEEN ELIZABETH
But thou didst kill my children.

KING RICHARD III
But in your daughter's womb I bury them:
Where in that nest of spicery they shall breed
Selves of themselves, to your recomforture.

QUEEN ELIZABETH
Shall I go win my daughter to thy will?

KING RICHARD III
And be a happy mother by the deed.

QUEEN ELIZABETH
I go. Write to me very shortly.
And you shall understand from me her mind.

KING RICHARD III
Bear her my true love's kiss; and so, farewell.

Exit QUEEN ELIZABETH

Relenting fool, and shallow, changing woman!

Enter RATCLIFF; CATESBY following

How now! what news?

RATCLIFF
My gracious sovereign, on the western coast
Rideth a puissant navy; to the shore
Throng many doubtful hollow-hearted friends,
Unarm'd, and unresolved to beat them back:
'Tis thought that Richmond is their admiral;
And there they hull, expecting but the aid
Of Buckingham to welcome them ashore.

KING RICHARD III
Some light-foot friend post to the Duke of Norfolk:
Ratcliff, thyself, or Catesby; where is he?

CATESBY
Here, my lord.

KING RICHARD III
Fly to the duke:

To RATCLIFF

Post thou to Salisbury
When thou comest thither—

To CATESBY

Dull, unmindful villain,
Why stand'st thou still, and go'st not to the duke?

CATESBY
First, mighty sovereign, let me know your mind,
What from your grace I shall deliver to him.

KING RICHARD III
O, true, good Catesby: bid him levy straight
The greatest strength and power he can make,
And meet me presently at Salisbury.

CATESBY
I go.

Exit

RATCLIFF
What is't your highness' pleasure I shall do at Salisbury?

KING RICHARD III

Why, what wouldst thou do there before I go?

RATCLIFF
Your highness told me I should post before.

KING RICHARD III
My mind is changed, sir, my mind is changed.

Enter STANLEY

How now, what news with you?

STANLEY
None good, my lord, to please you with the hearing;
Nor none so bad, but it may well be told.

KING RICHARD III
Hoyday, a riddle! neither good nor bad!
Why dost thou run so many mile about,
When thou mayst tell thy tale a nearer way?
Once more, what news?

STANLEY
Richmond is on the seas.

KING RICHARD III
There let him sink, and be the seas on him!
White-liver'd runagate, what doth he there?

STANLEY
I know not, mighty sovereign, but by guess.

KING RICHARD III
Well, sir, as you guess, as you guess?

STANLEY
Stirr'd up by Dorset, Buckingham, and Ely,
He makes for England, there to claim the crown.

KING RICHARD III
Is the chair empty? is the sword unsway'd?
Is the king dead? the empire unpossess'd?
What heir of York is there alive but we?
And who is England's king but great York's heir?
Then, tell me, what doth he upon the sea?

STANLEY
Unless for that, my liege, I cannot guess.

KING RICHARD III

Unless for that he comes to be your liege,
You cannot guess wherefore the Welshman comes.
Thou wilt revolt, and fly to him, I fear.

STANLEY
No, mighty liege; therefore mistrust me not.

KING RICHARD III
Where is thy power, then, to beat him back?
Where are thy tenants and thy followers?
Are they not now upon the western shore.
Safe-conducting the rebels from their ships!

STANLEY
No, my good lord, my friends are in the north.

KING RICHARD III
Cold friends to Richard: what do they in the north,
When they should serve their sovereign in the west?

STANLEY
They have not been commanded, mighty sovereign:
Please it your majesty to give me leave,
I'll muster up my friends, and meet your grace
Where and what time your majesty shall please.

KING RICHARD III
Ay, ay. thou wouldst be gone to join with Richmond:
I will not trust you, sir.

STANLEY
Most mighty sovereign,
You have no cause to hold my friendship doubtful:
I never was nor never will be false.

KING RICHARD III
Well,
Go muster men; but, hear you, leave behind
Your son, George Stanley: look your faith be firm.
Or else his head's assurance is but frail.

STANLEY
So deal with him as I prove true to you.

Exit

Enter a MESSENGER

MESSENGER
My gracious sovereign, now in Devonshire,
As I by friends am well advertised,

Sir Edward Courtney, and the haughty prelate
Bishop of Exeter, his brother there,
With many more confederates, are in arms.

Enter another MESSENGER

SECOND MESSENGER
My liege, in Kent the Guildfords are in arms;
And every hour more competitors
Flock to their aid, and still their power increaseth.

Enter another MESSENGER

THIRD MESSENGER
My lord, the army of the Duke of Buckingham—

KING RICHARD III
Out on you, owls! nothing but songs of death?
He striketh him
Take that, until thou bring me better news.

THIRD MESSENGER
The news I have to tell your majesty
Is, that by sudden floods and fall of waters,
Buckingham's army is dispersed and scatter'd;
And he himself wander'd away alone,
No man knows whither.

KING RICHARD III
I cry thee mercy:
There is my purse to cure that blow of thine.
Hath any well-advised friend proclaim'd
Reward to him that brings the traitor in?

THIRD MESSENGER
Such proclamation hath been made, my liege.

Enter another MESSENGER

FOURTH MESSENGER
Sir Thomas Lovel and Lord Marquis Dorset,
'Tis said, my liege, in Yorkshire are in arms.
Yet this good comfort bring I to your grace,
The Breton navy is dispersed by tempest:
Richmond, in Yorkshire, sent out a boat
Unto the shore, to ask those on the banks
If they were his assistants, yea or no;
Who answer'd him, they came from Buckingham.
Upon his party: he, mistrusting them,
Hoisted sail and made away for Brittany.

KING RICHARD III
March on, march on, since we are up in arms;
If not to fight with foreign enemies,
Yet to beat down these rebels here at home.

Re-enter CATESBY

CATESBY
My liege, the Duke of Buckingham is taken;
That is the best news: that the Earl of Richmond
Is with a mighty power landed at Milford,
Is colder tidings, yet they must be told.

KING RICHARD III
Away towards Salisbury! while we reason here,
A royal battle might be won and lost
Some one take order Buckingham be brought
To Salisbury; the rest march on with me.

Flourish.

Exeunt

SCENE V. Lord Derby's House

Enter DERBY and SIR CHRISTOPHER URSWICK

DERBY
Sir Christopher, tell Richmond this from me:
That in the sty of this most bloody boar
My son George Stanley is frank'd up in hold:
If I revolt, off goes young George's head;
The fear of that withholds my present aid.
But, tell me, where is princely Richmond now?

CHRISTOPHER
At Pembroke, or at Harford-west, in Wales.

DERBY
What men of name resort to him?

CHRISTOPHER
Sir Walter Herbert, a renowned soldier;
Sir Gilbert Talbot, Sir William Stanley;
Oxford, redoubted Pembroke, Sir James Blunt,
And Rice ap Thomas with a valiant crew;
And many more of noble fame and worth:
And towards London they do bend their course,
If by the way they be not fought withal.

DERBY
Return unto thy lord; commend me to him:
Tell him the queen hath heartily consented
He shall espouse Elizabeth her daughter.
These letters will resolve him of my mind. Farewell.

Exeunt

ACT V

SCENE I. Salisbury. An Open Place

Enter the SHERIFF, and BUCKINGHAM, with halberds, led to execution

BUCKINGHAM
Will not King Richard let me speak with him?

SHERIFF
No, my good lord; therefore be patient.

BUCKINGHAM
Hastings, and Edward's children, Rivers, Grey,
Holy King Henry, and thy fair son Edward,
Vaughan, and all that have miscarried
By underhand corrupted foul injustice,
If that your moody discontented souls
Do through the clouds behold this present hour,
Even for revenge mock my destruction!
This is All-Souls' day, fellows, is it not?

SHERIFF
It is, my lord.

BUCKINGHAM
Why, then All-Souls' day is my body's doomsday.
This is the day that, in King Edward's time,
I wish't might fall on me, when I was found
False to his children or his wife's allies
This is the day wherein I wish'd to fall
By the false faith of him I trusted most;
This, this All-Souls' day to my fearful soul
Is the determined respite of my wrongs:
That high All-Seer that I dallied with
Hath turn'd my feigned prayer on my head
And given in earnest what I begg'd in jest.
Thus doth he force the swords of wicked men
To turn their own points on their masters' bosoms:

Now Margaret's curse is fallen upon my head;
'When he,' quoth she, 'shall split thy heart with sorrow,
Remember Margaret was a prophetess.'
Come, sirs, convey me to the block of shame;
Wrong hath but wrong, and blame the due of blame.

Exeunt

SCENE II. The Camp Near Tamworth

Enter RICHMOND, OXFORD, BLUNT, HERBERT, and others, with drum and colours

RICHMOND
Fellows in arms, and my most loving friends,
Bruised underneath the yoke of tyranny,
Thus far into the bowels of the land
Have we march'd on without impediment;
And here receive we from our father Stanley
Lines of fair comfort and encouragement.
The wretched, bloody, and usurping boar,
That spoil'd your summer fields and fruitful vines,
Swills your warm blood like wash, and makes his trough
In your embowell'd bosoms, this foul swine
Lies now even in the centre of this isle,
Near to the town of Leicester, as we learn
From Tamworth thither is but one day's march.
In God's name, cheerly on, courageous friends,
To reap the harvest of perpetual peace
By this one bloody trial of sharp war.

OXFORD
Every man's conscience is a thousand swords,
To fight against that bloody homicide.

HERBERT
I doubt not but his friends will fly to us.

BLUNT
He hath no friends but who are friends for fear.
Which in his greatest need will shrink from him.

RICHMOND
All for our vantage. Then, in God's name, march:
True hope is swift, and flies with swallow's wings:
Kings it makes gods, and meaner creatures kings.

Exeunt

SCENE III. Bosworth Field

Enter KING RICHARD III in arms, with NORFOLK, SURREY, and others

KING RICHARD III
Here pitch our tents, even here in Bosworth field.
My Lord of Surrey, why look you so sad?

SURREY
My heart is ten times lighter than my looks.

KING RICHARD III
My Lord of Norfolk,—

NORFOLK
Here, most gracious liege.

KING RICHARD III
Norfolk, we must have knocks; ha! must we not?

NORFOLK
We must both give and take, my gracious lord.

KING RICHARD III
Up with my tent there! here will I lie tonight;
But where to-morrow? Well, all's one for that.
Who hath descried the number of the foe?

NORFOLK
Six or seven thousand is their utmost power.

KING RICHARD III
Why, our battalion trebles that account:
Besides, the king's name is a tower of strength,
Which they upon the adverse party want.
Up with my tent there! Valiant gentlemen,
Let us survey the vantage of the field
Call for some men of sound direction
Let's want no discipline, make no delay,
For, lords, to-morrow is a busy day.

Exeunt

Enter, on the other side of the field, RICHMOND, Sir William Brandon, OXFORD, and others. Some of the Soldiers pitch RICHMOND's tent

RICHMOND
The weary sun hath made a golden set,
And by the bright track of his fiery car,
Gives signal, of a goodly day to-morrow.

Sir William Brandon, you shall bear my standard.
Give me some ink and paper in my tent
I'll draw the form and model of our battle,
Limit each leader to his several charge,
And part in just proportion our small strength.
My Lord of Oxford, you, Sir William Brandon,
And you, Sir Walter Herbert, stay with me.
The Earl of Pembroke keeps his regiment:
Good Captain Blunt, bear my good night to him
And by the second hour in the morning
Desire the earl to see me in my tent:
Yet one thing more, good Blunt, before thou go'st,
Where is Lord Stanley quarter'd, dost thou know?

BLUNT
Unless I have mista'en his colours much,
Which well I am assured I have not done,
His regiment lies half a mile at least
South from the mighty power of the king.

RICHMOND
If without peril it be possible,
Good Captain Blunt, bear my good-night to him,
And give him from me this most needful scroll.

BLUNT
Upon my life, my lord, I'll under-take it;
And so, God give you quiet rest to-night!

RICHMOND
Good night, good Captain Blunt. Come gentlemen,
Let us consult upon to-morrow's business
In to our tent; the air is raw and cold.

They withdraw into the tent

Enter, to his tent, KING RICHARD III, NORFOLK, RATCLIFF, CATESBY, and others

KING RICHARD III
What is't o'clock?

CATESBY
It's supper-time, my lord;
It's nine o'clock.

KING RICHARD III
I will not sup to-night.
Give me some ink and paper.
What, is my beaver easier than it was?
And all my armour laid into my tent?

CATESBY
If is, my liege; and all things are in readiness.

KING RICHARD III
Good Norfolk, hie thee to thy charge;
Use careful watch, choose trusty sentinels.

NORFOLK
I go, my lord.

KING RICHARD III
Stir with the lark to-morrow, gentle Norfolk.

NORFOLK
I warrant you, my lord.

Exit

KING RICHARD III
Catesby!

CATESBY
My lord?

KING RICHARD III
Send out a pursuivant at arms
To Stanley's regiment; bid him bring his power
Before sunrising, lest his son George fall
Into the blind cave of eternal night.

Exit CATESBY

Fill me a bowl of wine. Give me a watch.
Saddle white Surrey for the field to-morrow.
Look that my staves be sound, and not too heavy.
Ratcliff!

RATCLIFF
My lord?

KING RICHARD III
Saw'st thou the melancholy Lord Northumberland?

RATCLIFF
Thomas the Earl of Surrey, and himself,
Much about cock-shut time, from troop to troop
Went through the army, cheering up the soldiers.

KING RICHARD III
So, I am satisfied. Give me a bowl of wine:
I have not that alacrity of spirit,

Nor cheer of mind, that I was wont to have.
Set it down. Is ink and paper ready?

RATCLIFF
It is, my lord.

KING RICHARD III
Bid my guard watch; leave me.
Ratcliff, about the mid of night come to my tent
And help to arm me. Leave me, I say.

Exeunt RATCLIFF and the other Attendants

Enter DERBY to RICHMOND in his tent, Lords and others attending

DERBY
Fortune and victory sit on thy helm!

RICHMOND
All comfort that the dark night can afford
Be to thy person, noble father-in-law!
Tell me, how fares our loving mother?

DERBY
I, by attorney, bless thee from thy mother
Who prays continually for Richmond's good:
So much for that. The silent hours steal on,
And flaky darkness breaks within the east.
In brief,—for so the season bids us be,—
Prepare thy battle early in the morning,
And put thy fortune to the arbitrament
Of bloody strokes and mortal-staring war.
I, as I may—that which I would I cannot,—
With best advantage will deceive the time,
And aid thee in this doubtful shock of arms:
But on thy side I may not be too forward
Lest, being seen, thy brother, tender George,
Be executed in his father's sight.
Farewell: the leisure and the fearful time
Cuts off the ceremonious vows of love
And ample interchange of sweet discourse,
Which so long sunder'd friends should dwell upon:
God give us leisure for these rites of love!
Once more, adieu: be valiant, and speed well!

RICHMOND
Good lords, conduct him to his regiment:
I'll strive, with troubled thoughts, to take a nap,
Lest leaden slumber peise me down to-morrow,
When I should mount with wings of victory:
Once more, good night, kind lords and gentlemen.

Exeunt all but RICHMOND

O Thou, whose captain I account myself,
Look on my forces with a gracious eye;
Put in their hands thy bruising irons of wrath,
That they may crush down with a heavy fall
The usurping helmets of our adversaries!
Make us thy ministers of chastisement,
That we may praise thee in the victory!
To thee I do commend my watchful soul,
Ere I let fall the windows of mine eyes:
Sleeping and waking, O, defend me still!

Sleeps

Enter the Ghost of PRINCE EDWARD, son to King Henry VI

Ghost of PRINCE EDWARD
[To **KING RICHARD III**]
Let me sit heavy on thy soul to-morrow!
Think, how thou stab'dst me in my prime of youth
At Tewksbury: despair, therefore, and die!
*To **RICHMOND***
Be cheerful, Richmond; for the wronged souls
Of butcher'd princes fight in thy behalf
King Henry's issue, Richmond, comforts thee.

Enter the Ghost of KING HENRY VI

Ghost of KING HENRY VI
[To **KING RICHARD III**]
When I was mortal, my anointed body
By thee was punched full of deadly holes
Think on the Tower and me: despair, and die!
Harry the Sixth bids thee despair, and die!

*To **RICHMOND***
Virtuous and holy, be thou conqueror!
Harry, that prophesied thou shouldst be king,
Doth comfort thee in thy sleep: live, and flourish!

Enter the Ghost of CLARENCE

Ghost of CLARENCE
[To **KING RICHARD III**]
Let me sit heavy on thy soul to-morrow!
I, that was wash'd to death with fulsome wine,
Poor Clarence, by thy guile betrayed to death!
To-morrow in the battle think on me,
And fall thy edgeless sword: despair, and die!

*To **RICHMOND***
Thou offspring of the house of Lancaster
The wronged heirs of York do pray for thee
Good angels guard thy battle! live, and flourish!

Enter the Ghosts of RIVERS, GRAY, and VAUGHAN

Ghost of RIVERS
[To **KING RICHARD III**]
Let me sit heavy on thy soul to-morrow,
Rivers. that died at Pomfret! despair, and die!

Ghost of GREY
[To **KING RICHARD III**]
Think upon Grey, and let thy soul despair!

Ghost of VAUGHAN
[To **KING RICHARD III**]
Think upon Vaughan, and, with guilty fear,
Let fall thy lance: despair, and die!

ALL
[To **RICHMOND**]
Awake, and think our wrongs in Richard's bosom
Will conquer him! awake, and win the day!

Enter the Ghost of HASTINGS

Ghost of HASTINGS
[To **KING RICHARD III**]
Bloody and guilty, guiltily awake,
And in a bloody battle end thy days!
Think on Lord Hastings: despair, and die!

To **RICHMOND**
Quiet untroubled soul, awake, awake!
Arm, fight, and conquer, for fair England's sake!

Enter the Ghosts of the two young Princes

Ghosts of YOUNG PRINCES
[To **KING RICHARD III**]
Dream on thy cousins smother'd in the Tower:
Let us be led within thy bosom, Richard,
And weigh thee down to ruin, shame, and death!
Thy nephews' souls bid thee despair and die!
To **RICHMOND**
Sleep, Richmond, sleep in peace, and wake in joy;
Good angels guard thee from the boar's annoy!

Live, and beget a happy race of kings!
Edward's unhappy sons do bid thee flourish.

Enter the Ghost of LADY ANNE

Ghost of LADY ANNE
[To **KING RICHARD III**]
Richard, thy wife, that wretched Anne thy wife,
That never slept a quiet hour with thee,
Now fills thy sleep with perturbations
To-morrow in the battle think on me,
And fall thy edgeless sword: despair, and die!

To **RICHMOND**
Thou quiet soul, sleep thou a quiet sleep
Dream of success and happy victory!
Thy adversary's wife doth pray for thee.

Enter the Ghost of BUCKINGHAM

Ghost of BUCKINGHAM
[To **KING RICHARD III**]
The last was I that helped thee to the crown;
The last was I that felt thy tyranny:
O, in the battle think on Buckingham,
And die in terror of thy guiltiness!
Dream on, dream on, of bloody deeds and death:
Fainting, despair; despairing, yield thy breath!

To **RICHMOND**
I died for hope ere I could lend thee aid:
But cheer thy heart, and be thou not dismay'd:
God and good angel fight on Richmond's side;
And Richard falls in height of all his pride.

The GHOSTS vanish

KING RICHARD III starts out of his dream

KING RICHARD III
Give me another horse: bind up my wounds.
Have mercy, Jesu!—Soft! I did but dream.
O coward conscience, how dost thou afflict me!
The lights burn blue. It is now dead midnight.
Cold fearful drops stand on my trembling flesh.
What do I fear? myself? there's none else by:
Richard loves Richard; that is, I am I.
Is there a murderer here? No. Yes, I am:
Then fly. What, from myself? Great reason why:
Lest I revenge. What, myself upon myself?
Alack. I love myself. Wherefore? for any good

That I myself have done unto myself?
O, no! alas, I rather hate myself
For hateful deeds committed by myself!
I am a villain: yet I lie. I am not.
Fool, of thyself speak well: fool, do not flatter.
My conscience hath a thousand several tongues,
And every tongue brings in a several tale,
And every tale condemns me for a villain.
Perjury, perjury, in the high'st degree
Murder, stem murder, in the direst degree;
All several sins, all used in each degree,
Throng to the bar, crying all, Guilty! guilty!
I shall despair. There is no creature loves me;
And if I die, no soul shall pity me:
Nay, wherefore should they, since that I myself
Find in myself no pity to myself?
Methought the souls of all that I had murder'd
Came to my tent; and every one did threat
To-morrow's vengeance on the head of Richard.

Enter RATCLIFF

RATCLIFF
My lord!

KING RICHARD III
'Zounds! who is there?

RATCLIFF
Ratcliff, my lord; 'tis I. The early village-cock
Hath twice done salutation to the morn;
Your friends are up, and buckle on their armour.

KING RICHARD III
O Ratcliff, I have dream'd a fearful dream!
What thinkest thou, will our friends prove all true?

RATCLIFF
No doubt, my lord.

KING RICHARD III
O Ratcliff, I fear, I fear,—

RATCLIFF
Nay, good my lord, be not afraid of shadows.

KING RICHARD III
By the apostle Paul, shadows to-night
Have struck more terror to the soul of Richard
Than can the substance of ten thousand soldiers
Armed in proof, and led by shallow Richmond.

It is not yet near day. Come, go with me;
Under our tents I'll play the eaves-dropper,
To see if any mean to shrink from me.

Exeunt

Enter the Lords to RICHMOND, sitting in his tent

LORDS
Good morrow, Richmond!

RICHMOND
Cry mercy, lords and watchful gentlemen,
That you have ta'en a tardy sluggard here.

LORDS
How have you slept, my lord?

RICHMOND
The sweetest sleep, and fairest-boding dreams
That ever enter'd in a drowsy head,
Have I since your departure had, my lords.
Methought their souls, whose bodies Richard murder'd,
Came to my tent, and cried on victory:
I promise you, my soul is very jocund
In the remembrance of so fair a dream.
How far into the morning is it, lords?

LORDS
Upon the stroke of four.

RICHMOND
Why, then 'tis time to arm and give direction.

His oration to his soldiers

More than I have said, loving countrymen,
The leisure and enforcement of the time
Forbids to dwell upon: yet remember this,
God and our good cause fight upon our side;
The prayers of holy saints and wronged souls,
Like high-rear'd bulwarks, stand before our faces;
Richard except, those whom we fight against
Had rather have us win than him they follow:
For what is he they follow? truly, gentlemen,
A bloody tyrant and a homicide;
One raised in blood, and one in blood establish'd;
One that made means to come by what he hath,
And slaughter'd those that were the means to help him;
Abase foul stone, made precious by the foil
Of England's chair, where he is falsely set;

One that hath ever been God's enemy:
Then, if you fight against God's enemy,
God will in justice ward you as his soldiers;
If you do sweat to put a tyrant down,
You sleep in peace, the tyrant being slain;
If you do fight against your country's foes,
Your country's fat shall pay your pains the hire;
If you do fight in safeguard of your wives,
Your wives shall welcome home the conquerors;
If you do free your children from the sword,
Your children's children quit it in your age.
Then, in the name of God and all these rights,
Advance your standards, draw your willing swords.
For me, the ransom of my bold attempt
Shall be this cold corpse on the earth's cold face;
But if I thrive, the gain of my attempt
The least of you shall share his part thereof.
Sound drums and trumpets boldly and cheerfully;
God and Saint George! Richmond and victory!

Exeunt

Re-enter KING RICHARD, RATCLIFF, Attendants and Forces

KING RICHARD III
What said Northumberland as touching Richmond?

RATCLIFF
That he was never trained up in arms.

KING RICHARD III
He said the truth: and what said Surrey then?

RATCLIFF
He smiled and said 'The better for our purpose.'

KING RICHARD III
He was in the right; and so indeed it is.

Clock striketh

Ten the clock there. Give me a calendar.
Who saw the sun to-day?

RATCLIFF
Not I, my lord.

KING RICHARD III
Then he disdains to shine; for by the book
He should have braved the east an hour ago
A black day will it be to somebody. Ratcliff!

RATCLIFF
My lord?

KING RICHARD III
The sun will not be seen to-day;
The sky doth frown and lour upon our army.
I would these dewy tears were from the ground.
Not shine to-day! Why, what is that to me
More than to Richmond? for the selfsame heaven
That frowns on me looks sadly upon him.

Enter NORFOLK

NORFOLK
Arm, arm, my lord; the foe vaunts in the field.

KING RICHARD III
Come, bustle, bustle; caparison my horse.
Call up Lord Stanley, bid him bring his power:
I will lead forth my soldiers to the plain,
And thus my battle shall be ordered:
My foreward shall be drawn out all in length,
Consisting equally of horse and foot;
Our archers shall be placed in the midst
John Duke of Norfolk, Thomas Earl of Surrey,
Shall have the leading of this foot and horse.
They thus directed, we will follow
In the main battle, whose puissance on either side
Shall be well winged with our chiefest horse.
This, and Saint George to boot! What think'st thou, Norfolk?

NORFOLK
A good direction, warlike sovereign.
This found I on my tent this morning.

He sheweth him a paper

KING RICHARD III
[Reads]
'Jockey of Norfolk, be not too bold,
For Dickon thy master is bought and sold.'
A thing devised by the enemy.
Go, gentleman, every man unto his charge
Let not our babbling dreams affright our souls:
Conscience is but a word that cowards use,
Devised at first to keep the strong in awe:
Our strong arms be our conscience, swords our law.
March on, join bravely, let us to't pell-mell
If not to heaven, then hand in hand to hell.

His oration to his Army

What shall I say more than I have inferr'd?
Remember whom you are to cope withal;
A sort of vagabonds, rascals, and runaways,
A scum of Bretons, and base lackey peasants,
Whom their o'er-cloyed country vomits forth
To desperate ventures and assured destruction.
You sleeping safe, they bring to you unrest;
You having lands, and blest with beauteous wives,
They would restrain the one, distain the other.
And who doth lead them but a paltry fellow,
Long kept in Bretagne at our mother's cost?
A milk-sop, one that never in his life
Felt so much cold as over shoes in snow?
Let's whip these stragglers o'er the seas again;
Lash hence these overweening rags of France,
These famish'd beggars, weary of their lives;
Who, but for dreaming on this fond exploit,
For want of means, poor rats, had hang'd themselves:
If we be conquer'd, let men conquer us,
And not these bastard Bretons; whom our fathers
Have in their own land beaten, bobb'd, and thump'd,
And in record, left them the heirs of shame.
Shall these enjoy our lands? lie with our wives?
Ravish our daughters?

Drum afar off

Hark! I hear their drum.
Fight, gentlemen of England! fight, bold yoemen!
Draw, archers, draw your arrows to the head!
Spur your proud horses hard, and ride in blood;
Amaze the welkin with your broken staves!

Enter a MESSENGER

What says Lord Stanley? will he bring his power?

MESSENGER
My lord, he doth deny to come.

KING RICHARD III
Off with his son George's head!

NORFOLK
My lord, the enemy is past the marsh
After the battle let George Stanley die.

KING RICHARD III

A thousand hearts are great within my bosom:
Advance our standards, set upon our foes
Our ancient word of courage, fair Saint George,
Inspire us with the spleen of fiery dragons!
Upon them! victory sits on our helms.

Exeunt

SCENE IV. Another Part of the Field.

Alarum: excursions. Enter NORFOLK and forces fighting; to him CATESBY

CATESBY
Rescue, my Lord of Norfolk, rescue, rescue!
The king enacts more wonders than a man,
Daring an opposite to every danger:
His horse is slain, and all on foot he fights,
Seeking for Richmond in the throat of death.
Rescue, fair lord, or else the day is lost!

Alarums.

Enter KING RICHARD III

KING RICHARD III
A horse! a horse! my kingdom for a horse!

CATESBY
Withdraw, my lord; I'll help you to a horse.

KING RICHARD III
Slave, I have set my life upon a cast,
And I will stand the hazard of the die:
I think there be six Richmonds in the field;
Five have I slain to-day instead of him.
A horse! a horse! my kingdom for a horse!

Exeunt

SCENE V. Another Part of the Field.

Alarum.

Enter KING RICHARD III and RICHMOND; they fight. KING RICHARD III is slain.

Retreat and flourish.

Re-enter RICHMOND, DERBY bearing the crown, with divers other LORDS

RICHMOND
God and your arms be praised, victorious friends,
The day is ours, the bloody dog is dead.

DERBY
Courageous Richmond, well hast thou acquit thee.
Lo, here, this long-usurped royalty
From the dead temples of this bloody wretch
Have I pluck'd off, to grace thy brows withal:
Wear it, enjoy it, and make much of it.

RICHMOND
Great God of heaven, say Amen to all!
But, tell me, is young George Stanley living?

DERBY
He is, my lord, and safe in Leicester town;
Whither, if it please you, we may now withdraw us.

RICHMOND
What men of name are slain on either side?

DERBY
John Duke of Norfolk, Walter Lord Ferrers,
Sir Robert Brakenbury, and Sir William Brandon.

RICHMOND
Inter their bodies as becomes their births:
Proclaim a pardon to the soldiers fled
That in submission will return to us:
And then, as we have ta'en the sacrament,
We will unite the white rose and the red:
Smile heaven upon this fair conjunction,
That long have frown'd upon their enmity!
What traitor hears me, and says not amen?
England hath long been mad, and scarr'd herself;
The brother blindly shed the brother's blood,
The father rashly slaughter'd his own son,
The son, compell'd, been butcher to the sire:
All this divided York and Lancaster,
Divided in their dire division,
O, now, let Richmond and Elizabeth,
The true succeeders of each royal house,
By God's fair ordinance conjoin together!
And let their heirs, God, if thy will be so.
Enrich the time to come with smooth-faced peace,
With smiling plenty and fair prosperous days!
Abate the edge of traitors, gracious Lord,
That would reduce these bloody days again,

And make poor England weep in streams of blood!
Let them not live to taste this land's increase
That would with treason wound this fair land's peace!
Now civil wounds are stopp'd, peace lives again:
That she may long live here, God say amen!

Exeunt

William Shakespeare – A Short Biography

The life of William Shakespeare, arguably the most significant figure in the Western literary canon, is relatively unknown. Even the exact date of his birth is uncertain. April 23rd, the date now generally accepted to be the date of his birth, is a result of a scholarly mistake and the appealing coincidence of its being also the day of his death.

That so little is known about a writer with such great literary scope and accomplishment has naturally invited speculation and conspiracy theories about the authenticity of his authorship, his influence and even his existence.

Shakespeare was born in Stratford-upon-Avon in 1565, possibly on the 23rd April, St. George's Day, and baptised there on 26th April. His father was John Shakespeare, a successful glover and alderman who hailed from Snitterfield. His mother was Mary Arden, whose father was an affluent landowner. In total their union bore eight children; William was the third of these and the eldest surviving son.

Although there is no hard evidence on his education it is widely agreed among scholars that William attended the King's New School in Stratford which was chartered as a free school in 1553. This school was only a quarter of a mile from the house in which he spent his childhood, but since there are no attendance records existing it is assumed, rather than known, this was the base for his education.

Although the quality of education in a grammar school at that time varied wildly the curriculum did not, a key aspect of which, by royal decree, was Latin, and it is undoubtable that the school will have delivered an intensive education in Latin grammar, drawing heavily on the work of the classical Latin authors. If Shakespeare did attend this school then it is very likely the starting point for the fascination with and extensive knowledge of the classical Latin authors which would inform and inspire so much of his work began.

Little more detail is known of William's childhood, or his early teenage years, until, at the age of 18, he married Anne Hathaway, who was 26 and from the nearby village of Shottery. Her father was a yeoman farmer, and their family home a small farmhouse in the village. In his will he left her £6 13s 4d, six pounds, thirteen shillings and fourpence, to be paid on her wedding day. On November 27th, 1582 the consistory court of the Diocese of Worcester issued a marriage licence, and on the 28th two of Hathaway's neighbours, Fulk Sandells and John Richardson, posted bonds which guaranteed that there were no lawful claims to impede the marriage along with a surety of £40 to act as a financial guarantee for the wedding.

The marriage was conducted in some haste since, unusually, the marriage banns were read only once instead of the more normal three times, a decision which would have been taken by the

Worcester chancellor. This haste is no doubt due to the child Anne delivered their first child, Susanna, six months later. Susanna, was baptised on May 26th, 1583. Several scholars have voiced their opinion that the wedding was imposed on a reluctant Shakespeare by Hathaway's outraged parents, although, again, there is nothing to formally support the theory. It has been further argued that the circumstances surrounding the wedding, particularly those of the neighbourly assurances, indicate that Shakespeare was involved with two women at the time of his marriage. According to the theory proposed by the early twentieth century scholar Frank Harris, Shakespeare had already chosen to marry a woman named Anne Whateley. It was only once this proposed union became known that Hathaway's outraged family forced him to marry their daughter. Harris goes on to surmise that Shakespeare considered the affair entrapment, and that this led to his wholesale despising of her, a "loathing for his wife [which] was measureless" and which ultimately caused him to leave Stratford and her and make for the theatre. But equally other scholars such as John Aubrey have responded to this with evidence that Shakespeare returned to Stratford every year which, if true, would rather diminish Harris's claim that Hathaway had poisoned Stratford for Shakespeare.

Harris's theory aside, Shakespeare and Hathaway had two more children, twins Hamnet and Judith, baptised on February 2nd,1585. Hamnet, Shakespeare's only son, died during one of the frequent outbreaks of bubonic plague and was buried on the August 11th, 1596, at the age of only eleven.

Little is known of Shakespeare's life during the years following the birth of the twins until he appears mentioned in relation to the London theatres in 1592, apart from a fleeting mention in the complaints bill of a legal case which came before the Queen's Bench court at Westminster, dated Michaelmas Term 1588 and October 9th, 1589. Despite this period of time being referred to in scholarly circles as Shakespeare's "lost years", there are several stories, apocryphal in nature, which are attributed to Shakespeare. For example, there is a legend in Stratford that he fled the town in order to avoid prosecution for poaching deer on the estate of Thomas Lucy, a local squire. It is also supposed that Shakespeare went so far as to take revenge on Lucy, a politician whose Protestantism opposed Shakespeare's Catholic childhood, by writing the following lampooning ballad about him:

> A parliament member, a justice of peace,
> At home a poor scarecrow, at London an ass,
> If lousy is Lucy as some folks miscall it
> Then Lucy is lousy whatever befall it.

However amusing the ballad and legend may be in imagining the life of a young Shakespeare, youthfully mischievous and still developing the wit, sense of adventure and humour which would become integral aspects of his writing, there is simply no evidence either to support the theory or to suggest that Shakespeare penned the ballad. Alongside this are suggestions that he began his theatrical career while minding the horses of the patrons of the London theatres and that he spent some time as a schoolmaster employed by one Alexander Hoghton, a Catholic landowner in Lancashire, in whose will is named "William Shakeshafte". However, this was a popular name in the Lancashire area at that time and there is no evidence that this referred to Shakespeare. The wealth of his writing makes it a frustrating exercise to learn more of his life and the manner in which he achieved those outstanding and lionized works.

Interestingly, the reference to Shakespeare in 1592 which ends the "lost years" is a piece of theatrical criticism by playwright Robert Greene in *Groats-Worth of Wit*. In a scathing passage Greene writes "...there is an upstart Crow, beautified with our feathers, that with his *Tiger's heart wrapped in a Player's hide*, supposes he is as well able to bombast out a blank verse as the best of you: and being an absolute *Johannes factotum*, is in his own conceit the only Shake-scene in a country." From this entry we can make some important inferences which shed light on

Shakespeare's career, the first of which is that to be acknowledged, even negatively, by a playwright such as Robert Greene, by this point he must have been making significant impact on the London stage as a writer. Also of significance is the very meaning of the words themselves, for it is generally acknowledged that Shakespeare is being accused of writing with a lofty ambition beyond his capabilities and, more importantly, the capabilities of his contemporaries who were educated at Oxford and Cambridge. Within this remark, then, is an inherent snobbery which Shakespeare would come to resent and ultimately challenge in his writing. Though Greene's parody of "Oh, tiger's heart wrapped in a woman's hide" makes reference to *Henry VI, Part 3*, it is likely that Greene's opinion of Shakespeare was in part informed by another of Shakespeare's plays which was heavily criticised, *Titus Adronicus*, believed to have been written between 1588 and 1593. It was his first attempt at tragedy, almost prototypical, and was written at a time when, according to the scholar Jonathan Bate, he was "experimenting with ways of writing about and representing rape and seduction". Drawing heavily on the sixth book of Ovid's *Metamorphoses* as its main source of inspiration for the rape and mutilation of Lavinia, it offended the sensibilities of the more highbrow members of its audience, whilst presumably also simultaneously intimidating them with its detailed knowledge of Ovid, a writer typically considered the reserve of the university-educated. Not only, then, was Shakespeare demonstrating a knowledge of classical literature which they thought befitted only a traditional scholar and thereby shining a light to the snobbery and exclusivity of such an education, but he was doing it radically and brilliantly.

By 1594 the Lord Chamberlain's Men had recognised his worthiness as a playwright and were performing his works. With the advantage of Shakespeare's progressive writing they rapidly became London's leading company of players, affording him more exposure and, following the death of Queen Elizabeth in 1603, a royal patent by the new king, James I, at which point they changed their name to the King's Men.

Before this success, though, several company members had formed a partnership to build their own theatre which came to be on the south bank of the river Thames, the now-famous and reconstructed Globe theatre. Though it is unclear precisely what Shakespeare's involvement in this venture was, records of his property and investments indicate that he came to be rich during this period, buying the second-largest house in Stratford, called New Place, in 1597, which he made his family home. Prior to this he was living in the parish of St Helen's Bishopsgate, north of the River Thames. He continued to spend most of his time at work in London and from about 1598-1602, he seems to have lived in the Paris Gardens area of Bankside south of the river near The Globe.

Despite efforts to pirate his work, Shakespeare's name was by 1598 so well known that it had already become a selling point in its own right on title pages.

An interesting aside is that theatres were mostly constructed on the south bank of the Thames (then part of the county of Surrey) as performing in London itself was thought to be a bad influence on the masses and subject to periodic bouts of censorship, repression and closing of venues which in the City itself was mainly courtyards and open areas at the many Inns.

Excluded from the City purpose built theatres began to be constructed outside the City limits. This area of the Thames though was rough and naturally vibrant with all sorts of characters, many of them of dubious nature or even criminal. It was also prone, due to its over-crowding and bad sanitation, to bouts of bubonic plague and other diseases particularly during the summer which was a further reason for the theatres there being closed. The Curtain, The Rose, The Swan, The Fortune, The Blackfriars and of course The Globe were all purpose built and situated here, some with an audience capacity approaching 3,000.

The first known printed copies of Shakespeare's plays date from 1594 in quarto editions, though these quarto editions are often considered "bad", a term referring to the likelihood of specific quarto editions being based on, for example, a reconstruction of a play as it was witnessed, rather than Shakespeare's original manuscript. The best example of such memorial reconstruction can be found in the differences between the first and second quarto editions of *Hamlet*. In examining Hamlet's most famous soliloquy, "to be or not to be", we can immediately recognise significant differences. First, the familiar second quarto version:

> To be, or not to be; that is the question:
> Whether 'tis nobler in the mind to suffer
> The slings and arrows of outrageous fortune,
> Or to take arms against a sea of troubles,
> And, by opposing, end them.

And, by contrast, the first quarto version:

> To be, or not to be, I there's the point,
> To Die, to sleep, is that all? I all:

For scholar Henry David Gray the first quarto lines are emblematic of "a distorted version of the completed drama filled out and revised by an inferior poet" and based, he goes on to argue, on the fractured memories of the play as witnessed and performed by the actor playing Marcellus. Gray, and several other critics, consider the first quarto a pirated copy, printed in haste without the writer's permission in an attempt to make quick money following the success of the play in the theatre. In understanding the significance of Marcellus to the theory it is imperative to note that the authenticity of each quarto is based on its similarities to the version of the play found in the first folio, printed in 1623 and believed to be authorised by Shakespeare. Therefore, since in the folio version of *Hamlet* the "to be or not to be" soliloquy is virtually identical to that of the second quarto, it is believed that the second was authored by Shakespeare himself and that the first, by its considerable differences, must therefore be in some way compromised. However, when read in comparison to the folio version, the only character whose lines are almost entirely perfect are those spoken by Marcellus, which, since dramatic practice at the time was for actors to be given only their own lines and three or four word 'cues' based on the lines preceding theirs, suggests that the first quarto is a memorial reconstruction of the play written by the actor who played Marcellus. Having committed his own lines to memory he was able to reproduce them accurately, but was left to fill in the remaining lines and plot from memory which accounts for the truncated and often vastly inferior writing in the first quarto.

According to the remaining cast lists from the period, Shakespeare remained an actor throughout his career as a writer, and it is thought he continued to act after he retired his pen. In 1616 he is recorded in the cast list in Ben Jonson's collected *Works* in the plays *Man in His Humour* 1598) and *Sejanus His Fall* (1603), though some scholars consider his absence from the list of Jonson's *Volpone* evidence that, by 1605, his acting career was nearing its end. Despite this in the First Folio he is listed as one of "the Principle Actors in all these Plays", several of which were only staged after *Volpone*.

By 1604 he had moved again, remaining north of the river, to an area near St. Paul's Cathedral where he rented a fine room amongst fine houses from Christopher Mountjoy, a French hatmaker and Huguenot.

The Anglo-Welsh poet John Davies of Hereford wrote in 1610 that "good Will" tended to play "kingly" roles, suggesting he was still on stage, perhaps now performing the more mature kings such as Lear and Henry VI. There has even been the suggestion that Shakespeare played the ghost of Hamlet's father, though there is little evidence to suggest it.

In 1608 the King's Men purchased the Blackfriars theatre from Henry Evans, and according to Cuthbert Burbage, one of the most highly regarded actors of the time, "placed many players" there "which were Heminges, Condell, Shakespeare, etc." A 1609 lawsuit brought against John Addenbrooke in Stratford on the 7th of June describes Shakespeare as "generosus nuper in curia domini Jacobi" (a gentleman recently at the court of King James) which indicates that by this time he was spending more time in Stratford. A likely cause of this was the bubonic plague, frequent outbreaks of which demanded the equally frequent closing of places of public gathering, principle among which were the theatres. Between May 1603 and February 1610 the theatres were closed for a total of 60 months, meaning there was no acting work and nobody to perform new plays. Though in 1610 Shakespeare returned to Stratford and it is supposed lived with his wife, he made frequent visits to London between 1611-14, being called as a witness in the trial *Bellott v. Mountjoy*, a case addressing concerns about the marriage settlement of Mountjoy's daughter, Mary. In March 1613 he purchased a gatehouse in the former Blackfriars priory, and spent several weeks in the city with his son-in-law John Hall, a physician, married to his daughter Susanna, from November 1614.

No plays are attributed to Shakespeare after 1613, and the last few plays he wrote before this time were in collaboration with other writers, one of whom is likely to be John Fletcher who succeeded him as the house playwright for the King's Men.

In early 1616 his daughter Judith married Thomas Quiney, a vintner and tobacconist. He signed his last will and testament on March 25th, of the same year, and the following day Quiney was ordered to do public penance for having fathered an illegitimate child with a woman named Margaret Wheeler who had died during childbirth which had enabled Quiney to cover up the scandal. This public humiliation would have been embarrassing for Shakespeare and his family.

William Shakespeare died two months later on April 23rd, 1616, survived by his wife and two daughters.

According to his will the bulk of his considerable estate was left to his elder daughter Susanna, with the instruction that she pass it down intact to "the first son of her body". However, though Susanna and Judith had four children between them they all died without progeny, ending Shakespeare's direct lineage. Also in his will was the instruction that his "second best bed" be left to his wife Anne, likely an insult, though the bed was possibly matrimonial and therefore of significant sentimental value.

He was buried two days after his death in the chancel of the Holy Trinity Church in Stratford-Upon-Avon.

The epitaph on the slab which covers his grave includes the following passage,

> Good frend for Iesvs sake forbeare,
> To digg the dvst enclosed heare.
> Bleste be ye man yt spares thes stones,
> And cvrst be he yt moves my bones

which, in modern translation, reads

> Good friend, for Jesus's sake forbear,
> To dig the dust enclosed here.
> Blessed be the man that spares these stones,
> And cursed be he that moves my bones.

At some point before 1623 there was a funerary monument erected in his memory on the north wall of Stratford-upon-Avon which features a half-effigy of him writing, and which likens him to Nestor, Socrates and Virgil.

On January 29th, 1741 a white marble memorial statue to him was erected in Poets' Corner in Westminster Abbey.

Though there have been many monuments built around the world in memory of Shakespeare, undoubtedly the greatest memorial of all is the body of work which became the foundation of Western literary canon and an inspiration for every generation.

William Shakespeare – A Concise Bibliography

1589	Comedy of Errors (Comedy)
1590	Henry VI, Part II (History)
	Henry VI, Part III (History)
1591	Henry VI, Part I (History)
1592	Richard III (History)
1593	Taming of the Shrew (Comedy)
	Titus Andronicus (Tragedy)
	Venus and Adonis (Poem)
1594	Rape of Lucrece (Poem)
	Romeo and Juliet (Tragedy)
	Two Gentlemen of Verona (Comedy)
	Love's Labour's Lost (Comedy)
1595	Richard II (History)
	Midsummer Night's Dream (Comedy)
1596	King John (History)
	Merchant of Venice (Comedy)
1597	Henry IV, Part I (History)
	Henry IV, Part II (History)
1598	Passionate Pilgrim (Poem)
	Henry V (History)
	Much Ado about Nothing (Comedy)

1599		Twelfth Night (Comedy)
		As You Like It (Comedy)
		Julius Caesar (Tragedy)
1600		Hamlet (Tragedy)
		Merry Wives of Windsor (Comedy)
1601		Troilus and Cressida (Comedy)
1601		Phoenix and the Turtle (Poem))
1602		All's Well That Ends Well (Comedy)
1604		Othello (Tragedy)
		Measure for Measure
1605		King Lear (Tragedy)
		Macbeth (Tragedy)
1606		Antony and Cleopatra (Tragedy)
1607		Coriolanus (Tragedy)
		Timon of Athens (Tragedy)
1608		Pericles (Comedy)
1609		Cymbeline (Comedy)
		Lover's Complaint (Poem)
1610		Winter's Tale (Comedy)
1611		Tempest (Comedy)
1612		Henry VIII (History)

As regards his 154 sonnets it is almost impossible to date each individually though collectively they were first published in 1609, with two having been published in 1599.

Shakspeare; or, the Poet by Ralph Waldo Emerson

Great (1) men are more distinguished by range and extent than by originality. If we require the originality which consists in weaving, like a spider, their web from their own bowels; in finding clay and making bricks and building the house; no great men are original. Nor does valuable originality consist in unlikeness to other men. The hero is in the press of knights and the thick of events; and seeing what men want and sharing their desire, he adds the needful length of sight and of arm, to come at the desired point. The greatest genius is the most indebted man. A poet is no rattle-brain, saying what comes uppermost, and, because he says every thing, saying at last something good; but a heart in unison with his time and country. There is nothing whimsical and fantastic in his production, but sweet and sad earnest, freighted with the weightiest convictions and pointed with the most determined aim which any man or class knows of in his times. (2)

The Genius of our life is jealous of individuals, and will not have any individual great, except through the general. There is no choice to genius. A great man does not wake up on some fine morning and say, 'I am full of life, I will go to sea and find an Antarctic continent: to-day I will square the circle: I will ransack botany and find a new food for man: I have a new architecture in my mind: I foresee a new mechanic power:' no, but he finds himself in the river of the thoughts and events, forced onward by the ideas and necessities of his contemporaries. (3) He stands where all the eyes of men look one way, and their hands all point in the direction in which he should go. The Church has reared him amidst rites and pomps, and he carries out the advice which her music gave him, and builds a cathedral needed by her chants and processions. He finds a war raging: it educates him, by trumpet, in barracks, and he betters the instruction. He finds two counties groping to bring coal, or flour, or fish, from the place of production to the place of consumption, and he hits on a railroad. Every master has found his materials collected, and his power lay in his sympathy with his people and in his love of the materials he wrought in. What an economy of power! and what a compensation for the shortness of life! All is done to his hand. The world has brought him thus far on his way. The human race has gone out before him, sunk the hills, filled the hollows and bridged the rivers. Men, nations, poets, artisans, women, all have worked for him, and he enters into their labors. Choose any other thing, out of the line of tendency, out of the national feeling and history, and he would have all to do for himself: his powers would be expended in the first preparations. Great genial power, one would almost say, consists in not being original at all; in being altogether receptive; in letting the world do all, and suffering the spirit of the hour to pass unobstructed through the mind. (4)

Shakspeare's youth fell in a time when the English people were importunate for dramatic entertainments. The court took offence easily at political allusions and attempted to suppress them. The Puritans, a growing and energetic party, and the religious among the Anglican church, would suppress them. But the people wanted them. Inn-yards, houses without roofs, and extemporaneous enclosures at country fairs were the ready theatres of strolling players. The people had tasted this new joy; and, as we could not hope to suppress newspapers now,—no, not by the strongest party,— neither then could king, prelate, or puritan, alone or united, suppress an organ which was ballad, epic, newspaper, caucus, lecture, Punch and library, at the same time. Probably king, prelate and puritan, all found their own account in it. It had become, by all causes, a national interest,—by no means conspicuous, so that some great scholar would have thought of treating it in an English history,—but not a whit less considerable because it was cheap and of no account, like a baker's-shop. The best proof of its vitality is the crowd of writers which suddenly broke into this field; Kyd, Marlow, Greene, Jonson, Chapman, Dekker, Webster, Heywood, Middleton, Peele, Ford, Massinger, Beaumont and Fletcher.

The secure possession, by the stage, of the public mind, is of the first importance to the poet who works for it. (5) He loses no time in idle experiments. Here is audience and expectation prepared. In the case of Shakspeare there is much more. At the time when he left Stratford and went up to London, a great body of stage-plays of all dates and writers existed in manuscript and were in turn produced on the boards. Here is the Tale of Troy, which the audience will bear hearing some part of, every week; the Death of Julius Cæsar, and other stories out of Plutarch, which they never tire of; a shelf full of English history, from the chronicles of Brut and Arthur, down to the royal Henries, which men hear eagerly; and a string of doleful tragedies, merry Italian tales and Spanish voyages, which all the London 'prentices know. All the mass has been treated, with more or less skill, by every playwright, and the prompter has the soiled and tattered manuscripts. It is now no longer possible to say who wrote them first. They have been the property of the Theatre so long, and so many rising geniuses have enlarged or altered them, inserting a speech or a whole scene, or adding a song, that no man can any longer claim copyright in this work of numbers. Happily, no man wishes to. They are not yet desired in that way. We have few readers, many spectators and hearers. They had best lie where they are.

Shakspeare, in common with his comrades, esteemed the mass of old plays waste stock, in which any experiment could be freely tried. Had the prestige which hedges about a modern tragedy existed, nothing could have been done. The rude warm blood of the living England circulated in the play, as in street-ballads, and gave body which he wanted to his airy and majestic fancy. The poet needs a ground in popular tradition on which he may work, and which, again, may restrain his art within the due temperance. It holds him to the people, supplies a foundation for his edifice, and in furnishing so much work done to his hand, leaves him at leisure and in full strength for the audacities of his imagination. In short, the poet owes to his legend what sculpture owed to the temple. Sculpture in Egypt and in Greece grew up in subordination to architecture. It was the ornament of the temple wall: at first a rude relief carved on pediments, then the relief became bolder and a head or arm was projected from the wall; the groups being still arranged with reference to the building, which serves also as a frame to hold the figures; and when at last the greatest freedom of style and treatment was reached, the prevailing genius of architecture still enforced a certain calmness and continence in the statue. As soon as the statue was begun for itself, and with no reference to the temple or palace, the art began to decline: freak, extravagance and exhibition took the place of the old temperance. This balance-wheel, which the sculptor found in architecture, the perilous irritability of poetic talent found in the accumulated dramatic materials to which the people were already wonted, and which had a certain excellence which no single genius, however extraordinary, could hope to create.

In point of fact it appears that Shakspeare did owe debts in all directions, and was able to use whatever he found; and the amount of indebtedness may be inferred from Malone's laborious computations in regard to the First, Second and Third parts of Henry VI., in which, "out of 6043 lines, 1771 were written by some author preceding Shakspeare, 2373 by him, on the foundation laid by his predecessors, and 1899 were entirely his own." And the proceeding investigation hardly leaves a single drama of his absolute invention. Malone's sentence is an important piece of external history. In Henry VIII. I think I see plainly the cropping out of the original rock on which his own finer stratum was laid. The first play was written by a superior, thoughtful man, with a vicious ear. I can mark his lines, and know well their cadence. See Wolsey's soliloquy, and the following scene with Cromwell, where instead of the metre of Shakspeare, whose secret is that the thought constructs the tune, so that reading for the sense will best bring out the rhythm,—here the lines are constructed on a given tune, and the verse has even a trace of pulpit eloquence. But the play contains through all its length unmistakable traits of Shakspeare's hand, and some passages, as the account of the coronation, are like autographs. What is odd, the compliment to Queen Elizabeth is in the bad rhythm. (6)

Shakspeare knew that tradition supplies a better fable than any invention can. If he lost any credit of design, he augmented his resources; and, at that day, our petulant demand for originality was not so much pressed. There was no literature for the million. The universal reading, the cheap press, were unknown. A great poet who appears in illiterate times, absorbs into his sphere all the light which is any where radiating. Every intellectual jewel, every flower of sentiment it is his fine office to bring to his people; and he comes to value his memory equally with his invention. (7) He is therefore little solicitous whence his thoughts have been derived; whether through translation, whether through tradition, whether by travel in distant countries, whether by inspiration; from whatever source, they are equally welcome to his uncritical audience. Nay, he borrows very near home. Other men say wise things as well as he; only they say a good many foolish things, and do not know when they have spoken wisely. He knows the sparkle of the true stone, and puts it in high place, wherever he finds it. (8) Such is the happy position of Homer perhaps; of Chaucer, of Saadi. They felt that all wit was their wit. And they are librarians and historiographers, as well as poets. Each romancer was heir and dispenser of all the hundred tales of the world,—

"Presenting Thebes' and Pelops' line
And the tale of Troy divine." (9)

The influence of Chaucer is conspicuous in all our early literature; and more recently not only Pope and Dryden have been beholden to him, but, in the whole society of English writers, a large unacknowledged debt is easily traced. One is charmed with the opulence which feeds so many pensioners. But Chaucer is a huge borrower. Chaucer, it seems, drew continually, through Lydgate and Caxton, from Guido di Colonna, whose Latin romance of the Trojan war was in turn a compilation from Dares Phrygius, Ovid and Statius. Then Petrarch, Boccaccio and the Provençal poets are his benefactors: the Romaunt of the Rose is only judicious translation from William of Lorris and John of Meung: Troilus and Creseide, from Lollius of Urbino: The Cock and the Fox, from the Lais of Marie: The House of Fame, from the French or Italian: and poor Gower he uses as if he were only a brick-kiln or stone-quarry out of which to build his house. (10) He steals by this apology,—that what he takes has no worth where he finds it and the greatest where he leaves it. It has come to be practically a sort of rule in literature, that a man having once shown himself capable of original writing, is entitled thenceforth to steal from the writings of others at discretion. Thought is the property of him who can entertain it and of him who can adequately place it. A certain awkwardness marks the use of borrowed thoughts; but as soon as we have learned what to do with them they become our own.

Thus all originality is relative. Every thinker is retrospective. The learned member of the legislature, at Westminster or at Washington, speaks and votes for thousands. Show us the constituency, and the now invisible channels by which the senator is made aware of their wishes; the crowd of practical and knowing men, who, by correspondence or conversation, are feeding him with evidence, anecdotes and estimates, and it will bereave his fine attitude and resistance of something of their impressiveness. As Sir Robert Peel and Mr. Webster vote, so Locke and Rousseau think, for thousands; and so there were fountains all around Homer, (11) Menu, Saadi, or Milton, from which they drew; friends, lovers, books, traditions, proverbs,—all perished—which, if seen, would go to reduce the wonder. Did the bard speak with authority? Did he feel himself overmatched by any companion? The appeal is to the consciousness of the writer. Is there at last in his breast a Delphi whereof to ask concerning any thought or thing, whether it be verily so, yea or nay? and to have answer, and to rely on that? All the debts which such a man could contract to other wit would never disturb his consciousness of originality; for the ministrations of books and of other minds are a whiff of smoke to that most private reality with which he has conversed. (12)

It is easy to see that what is best written or done by genius in the world, was no man's work, but came by wide social labor, when a thousand wrought like one, sharing the same impulse. Our English Bible is a wonderful specimen of the strength and music of the English language. But it was not made by one man, or at one time; but centuries and churches brought it to perfection. There never was a time when there was not some translation existing. The Liturgy, admired for its energy and pathos, is an anthology of the piety of ages and nations, a translation of the prayers and forms of the Catholic church,—these collected, too, in long periods, from the prayers and meditations of every saint and sacred writer all over the world. (13) Grotius makes the like remark in respect to the Lord's Prayer, that the single clauses of which it is composed were already in use in the time of Christ, in the Rabbinical forms. He picked out the grains of gold. The nervous language of the Common Law, the impressive forms of our courts and the precision and substantial truth of the legal distinctions, are the contribution of all the sharp-sighted, strong-minded men who have lived in the countries where these laws govern. The translation of Plutarch gets its excellence by being translation on translation.

There never was a time when there was none. All the truly idiomatic and national phrases are kept, and all others successively picked out and thrown away. Something like the same process had gone on, long before, with the originals of these books. The world takes liberties with world-books. Vedas, Æsop's Fables, Pilpay, Arabian Nights, Cid, Iliad, Robin Hood, Scottish Minstrelsy, are not the work of single men. In the composition of such works the time thinks, the market thinks, the mason, the carpenter, the merchant, the farmer, the fop, all think for us. Every book supplies its time with one good word; every municipal law, every trade, every folly of the day; and the generic catholic genius who is not afraid or ashamed to owe his originality to the originality of all, stands with the next age as the recorder and embodiment of his own. (14)

We have to thank the researches of antiquaries, and the Shakspeare Society, for ascertaining the steps of the English drama, from the Mysteries celebrated in churches and by churchmen, and the final detachment from the church, and the completion of secular plays, from Ferrex and Porrex, (15) and Gammer Gurton's Needle, down to the possession of the stage by the very pieces which Shakspeare altered, remodelled and finally made his own. Elated with success and piqued by the growing interest of the problem, they have left no bookstall unsearched, no chest in a garret unopened, no file of old yellow accounts to decompose in damp and worms, so keen was the hope to discover whether the boy Shakspeare poached or not, whether he held horses at the theatre door, whether he kept school, and why he left in his will only his second-best bed to Ann Hathaway, his wife.

There is somewhat touching in the madness with which the passing age mischooses the object on which all candles shine and all eyes are turned; the care with which it registers every trifle touching Queen Elizabeth and King James, and the Essexes, Leicesters, Burleighs and Buckinghams; and lets pass without a single valuable note the founder of another dynasty, which alone will cause the Tudor dynasty to be remembered,—the man who carries the Saxon race in him by the inspiration which feeds him, and on whose thoughts the foremost people of the world are now for some ages to be nourished, and minds to receive this and not another bias. A popular player;—nobody suspected he was the poet of the human race; and the secret was kept as faithfully from poets and intellectual men as from courtiers and frivolous people. (16) Bacon, who took the inventory of the human understanding for his times, never mentioned his name. Ben Jonson, though we have strained his few words of regard and panegyric, had no suspicion of the elastic fame whose first vibrations he was attempting. He no doubt thought the praise he has conceded to him generous, and esteemed himself, out of all question, the better poet of the two.

If it need wit to know wit, according to the proverb, Shakspeare's time should be capable of recognizing it. Sir Henry Wotton was born four years after Shakspeare, and died twenty-three years after him; and I find, among his correspondents and acquaintances, the following persons: Theodore Beza, Isaac Casaubon, Sir Philip Sidney, the Earl of Essex, Lord Bacon, Sir Walter Raleigh, John Milton, Sir Henry Vane, Isaac Walton, Dr. Donne, Abraham Cowley, Bellarmine, Charles Cotton, John Pym, John Hales, Kepler, Vieta, Albericus Gentilis, Paul Sarpi, Arminius; with all of whom exists some token of his having communicated, without enumerating many others whom doubtless he saw,— Shakspeare, Spenser, Jonson, Beaumont, Massinger, the two Herberts, Marlow, Chapman and the rest. Since the constellation of great men who appeared in Greece in the time of Pericles, there was never any such society;—yet their genius failed them to find out the best head in the universe. (17) Our poet's mask was impenetrable. You cannot see the mountain near. It took a century to make it suspected; and not until two centuries had passed, after his death, did any criticism which we think adequate begin to appear. It was not possible to write the history of Shakspeare till now; for he is the father of German literature: it was with the introduction of Shakspeare into German, by Lessing, and the translation of his works by Wieland and Schlegel, that the rapid burst of German literature was most intimately connected. It was not until the nineteenth century, whose speculative genius is a sort of living Hamlet, that the tragedy of Hamlet could find such wondering readers. (18) Now, literature, philosophy and thought are Shakspearized. His mind is the horizon beyond which, at present, we do not see. Our ears are educated to music by his rhythm. Coleridge and Goethe are the only critics who have expressed our convictions with any adequate fidelity: but there is in all cultivated minds a silent appreciation of his superlative power and beauty, which, like Christianity, qualifies the period.

The Shakspeare Society have inquired in all directions, advertised the missing facts, offered money for any information that will lead to proof,—and with what result? Beside some important illustration of the history of the English stage, to which I have adverted, they have gleaned a few facts touching the property, and dealings in regard to property, of the poet. It appears that from year to year he owned a larger share in the Blackfriars' Theatre: its wardrobe and other appurtenances were his: that he bought an estate in his native village with his earnings as writer and shareholder; that he lived in the best house in Stratford; was intrusted by his neighbors with their commissions in London, as of borrowing money, and the like; that he was a veritable farmer. About the time when he was writing Macbeth, he sues Philip Rogers, in the borough-court of Stratford, for thirty-five shillings, ten pence, for corn delivered to him at different times; and in all respects appears as a good husband, with no reputation for eccentricity or excess. He was a good-natured sort of man, an actor and shareholder in the theatre, not in any striking manner distinguished from other actors and managers. (19) I admit the importance of this information. It was well worth the pains that have been taken to procure it.

But whatever scraps of information concerning his condition these researches may have rescued, they can shed no light upon that infinite invention which is the concealed magnet of his attraction for us. We are very clumsy writers of history. We tell the chronicle of parentage, birth, birth-place, schooling, school-mates, earning of money, marriage, publication of books, celebrity, death; and when we have come to an end of this gossip, no ray of relation appears between it and the goddess-born; and it seems as if, had we dipped at random into the "Modern Plutarch," and read any other life there, it would have fitted the poems as well. (20) It is the essence of poetry to spring, like the rainbow daughter of Wonder, from the invisible, to abolish the past and refuse all history. Malone, Warburton, Dyce and Collier have wasted their oil. The famed theatres, Covent Garden, Drury Lane, the Park and Tremont have vainly assisted. Betterton, Garrick, Kemble, Kean and Macready dedicate their lives to this genius; him they crown, elucidate, obey and express. The genius knows them not. The recitation begins; one golden word leaps out immortal from all this painted pedantry and sweetly torments us with invitations to its own inaccessible homes. I remember I went once to see the Hamlet of a famed performer, the pride of the English stage; and all I then heard and all I now remember of the tragedian was that in which the tragedian had no part; simply Hamlet's question to the ghost:—

"What may this mean,
That thou, dead corse, again in complete steel
Revisit'st thus the glimpses of the moon?"

That imagination which dilates the closet he writes in to the world's dimension, crowds it with agents in rank and order, as quickly reduces the big reality to be the glimpses of the moon. (21) These tricks of his magic spoil for us the illusions of the green-room. Can any biography shed light on the localities into which the Midsummer Night's Dream admits me? Did Shakspeare confide to any notary or parish recorder, sacristan, or surrogate in Stratford, the genesis of that delicate creation? The forest of Arden, the nimble air of Scone Castle, the moonlight of Portia's villa, "the antres vast and desarts idle" of Othello's captivity,—where is the third cousin, or grand-nephew, the chancellor's file of accounts, or private letter, that has kept one word of those transcendent secrets?

In fine, in this drama, as in all great works of art,—in the Cyclopæan architecture of Egypt and India, in the Phidian sculpture, the Gothic minsters, the Italian painting, the Ballads of Spain and Scotland,—the Genius draws up the ladder after him, when the creative age goes up to heaven, and gives way to a new age, which sees the works and asks in vain for a history.

Shakspeare is the only biographer of Shakspeare; and even he can tell nothing, except to the Shakspeare in us, that is, to our most apprehensive and sympathetic hour. (22) He cannot step from off his tripod and give us anecdotes of his inspirations. Read the antique documents extricated, analyzed and compared by the assiduous Dyce and Collier, and now read one of these skyey sentences,—aerolites,—which seem to have fallen out of heaven, and which not your experience but the man within the breast has accepted as words of fate, and tell me if they match; if the former account in any manner for the latter; or which gives the most historical insight into the man.

Hence, though our external history is so meagre, yet, with Shakspeare for biographer, instead of Aubrey and Rowe, we have really the information which is material; that which describes character and fortune, that which, if we were about to meet the man and deal with him, would most import us to know. We have his recorded convictions on those questions which knock for answer at every heart,—on life and death, on love, on wealth and poverty, on the prizes of life and the ways whereby we come at them; on the characters of men, and the influences, occult and open, which affect their fortunes; and on those mysterious and demoniacal powers which defy our science and which yet interweave their malice and their gift in our brightest hours. Who ever read the volume of the Sonnets without finding that the poet had there revealed, under masks that are no masks to the intelligent, the lore of friendship and of love; the confusion of sentiments in the most susceptible, and, at the same time, the most intellectual of men? What trait of his private mind has he hidden in his dramas? One can discern, in his ample pictures of the gentleman and the king, what forms and humanities pleased him; his delight in troops of friends, in large hospitality, in cheerful giving. Let Timon, let Warwick, let Antonio the merchant answer for his great heart. So far from Shakspeare's being the least known, he is the one person, in all modern history, known to us. What point of morals, of manners, of economy, of philosophy, of religion, of taste, of the conduct of life, has he not settled? What mystery has he not signified his knowledge of? What office, or function, or district of man's work, has he not remembered? What king has he not taught state, as Talma taught Napoleon? What maiden has not found him finer than her delicacy? What lover has he not outloved? What sage has he not outseen? What gentleman has he not instructed in the rudeness of his behavior?

Some able and appreciating critics think no criticism on Shakspeare valuable that does not rest purely on the dramatic merit; that he is falsely judged as poet and philosopher. I think as highly as these critics of his dramatic merit, but still think it secondary. He was a full man, who liked to talk; a brain exhaling thoughts and images, which, seeking vent, found the drama next at hand. (23) Had he been less, we should have had to consider how well he filled his place, how good a dramatist he was,—and he is the best in the world. But it turns out that what he has to say is of that weight as to withdraw some attention from the vehicle; and he is like some saint whose history is to be rendered into all languages, into verse and prose, into songs and pictures, and cut up into proverbs; so that the occasion which gave the saint's meaning the form of a conversation, or of a prayer, or of a code of laws, is immaterial compared with the universality of its application. So it fares with the wise Shakspeare and his book of life. He wrote the airs for all our modern music: he wrote the text of modern life; the text of manners: he drew the man of England and Europe; the father of the man in America; (24) he drew the man, and described the day, and what is done in it: he read the hearts of men and women, their probity, and their second thought and wiles; the wiles of innocence, and the transitions by which virtues and vices slide into their contraries: he could divide the mother's part from the father's part in the face of the child, or draw the fine demarcations of freedom and of fate:

he knew the laws of repression which make the police of nature: and all the sweets and all the terrors of human lot lay in his mind as truly but as softly as the landscape lies on the eye. And the importance of this wisdom of life sinks the form, as of Drama or Epic, out of notice. 'T is like making a question concerning the paper on which a king's message is written.

Shakspeare is as much out of the category of eminent authors, as he is out of the crowd. He is inconceivably wise; the others, conceivably. A good reader can, in a sort, nestle into Plato's brain and think from thence; but not into Shakspeare's. We are still out of doors. For executive faculty, for creation, Shakspeare is unique. No man can imagine it better. He was the farthest reach of subtlety compatible with an individual self,—the subtlest of authors, and only just within the possibility of authorship. (25) With this wisdom of life is the equal endowment of imaginative and of lyric power. He clothed the creatures of his legend with form and sentiments as if they were people who had lived under his roof; and few real men have left such distinct characters as these fictions. And they spoke in language as sweet as it was fit. Yet his talents never seduced him into an ostentation, nor did he harp on one string. An omnipresent humanity co-ordinates all his faculties. Give a man of talents a story to tell, and his partiality will presently appear. He has certain observations, opinions, topics, which have some accidental prominence, and which he disposes all to exhibit. He crams this part and starves that other part, consulting not the fitness of the thing, but his fitness and strength. But Shakspeare has no peculiarity, no importunate topic; but all is duly given; no veins, no curiosities; no cow-painter, no bird-fancier, no mannerist is he: he has no discoverable egotism: the great he tells greatly; the small subordinately. He is wise without emphasis or assertion; he is strong, as nature is strong, who lifts the land into mountain slopes without effort and by the same rule as she floats a bubble in the air, and likes as well to do the one as the other. This makes that equality of power in farce, tragedy, narrative, and love-songs; a merit so incessant that each reader is incredulous of the perception of other readers.

This power of expression, or of transferring the inmost truth of things into music and verse, makes him the type of the poet and has added a new problem to metaphysics. This is that which throws him into natural history, as a main production of the globe, and as announcing new eras and ameliorations. Things were mirrored in his poetry without loss or blur: he could paint the fine with precision, the great with compass, the tragic and the comic indifferently and without any distortion or favor. He carried his powerful execution into minute details, to a hair point; finishes an eyelash or a dimple as firmly as he draws a mountain; and yet these, like nature's, will bear the scrutiny of the solar microscope.

In short, he is the chief example to prove that more or less of production, more or fewer pictures, is a thing indifferent. He had the power to make one picture. Daguerre learned how to let one flower etch its image on his plate of iodine, and then proceeds at leisure to etch a million. There are always objects; but there was never representation. Here is perfect representation, at last; and now let the world of figures sit for their portraits. No recipe can be given for the making of a Shakspeare; but the possibility of the translation of things into song is demonstrated.

His lyric power lies in the genius of the piece. The sonnets, though their excellence is lost in the splendor of the dramas, are as inimitable as they; and it is not a merit of lines, but a total merit of the piece; like the tone of voice of some incomparable person, so is this a speech of poetic beings, and any clause as unproducible now as a whole poem.

Though the speeches in the plays, and single lines, have a beauty which tempts the ear to pause on them for their euphuism, yet the sentence is so loaded with meaning and so linked with its foregoers and followers, that the logician is satisfied. His means are as admirable as his ends; every subordinate invention, by which he helps himself to connect some irreconcilable opposites, is a poem too. He is not reduced to dismount and walk because his horses are running off with him in some distant direction: he always rides.

The finest poetry was first experience; but the thought has suffered a transformation since it was an experience. Cultivated men often attain a good degree of skill in writing verses; but it is easy to read, through their poems, their personal history: any one acquainted with the parties can name every figure; this is Andrew and that is Rachel. The sense thus remains prosaic. It is a caterpillar with wings, and not yet a butterfly. In the poet's mind the fact has gone quite over into the new element of thought, and has lost all that is exuvial. This generosity abides with Shakespeare. We say, from the truth and closeness of his pictures, that he knows the lesson by heart. Yet there is not a trace of egotism.

One more royal trait properly belongs to the poet. I mean his cheerfulness, without which no man can be a poet,—for beauty is his aim. He loves virtue, not for its obligation but for its grace: he delights in the world, in man, in woman, for the lovely light that sparkles from them. Beauty, the spirit of joy and hilarity, he sheds over the universe. Epicurus relates that poetry hath such charms that a lover might forsake his mistress to partake of them. And the true bards have been noted for their firm and cheerful temper. Homer lies in sunshine; Chaucer is glad and erect; and Saadi says, "It was rumored abroad that I was penitent; but what had I to do with repentance?" (26) Not less sovereign and cheerful,—much more sovereign and cheerful, is the tone of Shakespeare. His name suggests joy and emancipation to the heart of men. If he should appear in any company of human souls, who would not march in his troop? He touches nothing that does not borrow health and longevity from his festal style.

And now, how stands the account of man with this bard and benefactor, when, in solitude, shutting our ears to the reverberations of his fame, we seek to strike the balance? Solitude has austere lessons; it can teach us to spare both heroes and poets; and it weighs Shakespeare also, and finds him to share the halfness and imperfection of humanity.

Shakespeare, Homer, Dante, Chaucer, saw the splendor of meaning that plays over the visible world; knew that a tree had another use than for apples, and corn another than for meal, and the ball of the earth, than for tillage and roads: that these things bore a second and finer harvest to the mind, being emblems of its thoughts, and conveying in all their natural history a certain mute commentary on human life. (27) Shakespeare employed them as colors to compose his picture. He rested in their beauty; and never took the step which seemed inevitable to such genius, namely to explore the virtue which resides in these symbols and imparts this power:—what is that which they themselves say? He converted the elements which waited on his command, into entertainments. He was master of the revels to mankind. Is it not as if one should have, through majestic powers of science, the comets given into his hand, or the planets and their moons, and should draw them from their orbits to glare with the municipal fireworks on a holiday night, and advertise in all towns, "Very superior pyrotechny this evening"? Are the agents of nature, and the power to understand them, worth no more than a street serenade, or the breath of a cigar? One remembers again the trumpet-text in the Koran,—"The heavens and the earth and all that is between them, think ye we have created them in jest?" As long as the question is of talent and mental power, the world of men has not his equal to show. But when the question is, to life and its materials and its auxiliaries, how does he profit me? What does it signify? It is but a Twelfth Night, or Midsummer-Night's Dream, or Winter Evening's Tale: what signifies another picture more or less? The Egyptian verdict of the Shakespeare Societies comes to mind; that he was a jovial actor and manager. I can not marry this fact to his verse. Other admirable men have led lives in some sort of keeping with their thought; but this man, in wide contrast. Had he been less, had he reached only the common measure of great authors, of Bacon, Milton, Tasso, Cervantes, we might leave the fact in the twilight of human fate: but that this man of men, he who gave to the science of mind a new and larger subject than had ever existed, and planted the standard of humanity some furlongs forward into Chaos,—that he should not be wise for himself;—it must even go into the world's history that the best poet led an obscure and profane life, using his genius for the public amusement. (28)

Well, other men, priest and prophet, Israelite, German and Swede, beheld the same objects: they also saw through them that which was contained. And to what purpose? The beauty straightway vanished; they read commandments, all-excluding mountainous duty; an obligation, a sadness, as of piled mountains, fell on them, and life became ghastly, joyless, a pilgrim's progress, a probation, beleaguered round with doleful histories of Adam's fall and curse behind us; with doomsdays and purgatorial and penal fires before us; and the heart of the seer and the heart of the listener sank in them.

It must be conceded that these are half-views of half-men. The world still wants its poet-priest, a reconciler, who shall not trifle, with Shakespeare the player, nor shall grope in graves, with Swedenborg the mourner; but who shall see, speak, and act, with equal inspiration. For knowledge will brighten the sunshine; right is more beautiful than private affection; and love is compatible with universal wisdom. (29)

Footnotes

Note 1.

This essay was read as a lecture in Exeter Hall, in London, in June, 1848.

Perhaps it is well to bear in mind that Mr. Emerson was reared for the ministry and ordained a clergyman, and that his ancestors for several generations had exercised that office, and moreover that, in New England, up to his day, theatrical representations had been looked at with disfavor by serious and God-fearing people, and the witnessing of such by a minister would, like dancing, have been considered unbecoming indulgence. Although Mr. Emerson emancipated himself from bonds that were merely professional or artificial, he had an inbred distaste for the common amusements of society, feeling that they were unbecoming to a scholar, and that he was not adapted for them, though he was tolerant of them in other people. There was a natural earnestness, and a simple and cheerful asceticism in his early and later life. Yet once in his later life, when he had been induced to go to see Mr. and Mrs. Barney Williams in some bright comedy, he praised their acting and admitted to his daughter that he really much enjoyed theatrical performances, in spite of the feeling that they were not for him. Dancing, for instance, which he considered a proper part of youths' education, would have seemed unbecoming for himself. He says, "It shall be writ in my memoirs ... as it was writ of St. Pachonius, Pes ejus ad saltandum non est commotus omni vita sua." His staying away from theatrical entertainments was instinctive, but he was liberal in the matter and would go to see a real artist. He even went to see the performance of the beautiful dancer Fanny Elssler, although a story which has been too often repeated of his remarks to Margaret Fuller on the subject is as false as it is silly.

In Paris he saw Rachel during the Revolution of 1848, and often told his children of her fierce and splendid declamation of the Marseillaise in the theatre, holding the tricolor aloft. On London in that same year he wrote of seeing Macready in Lear, with Mrs. Butler as Cordelia. It was to see one of Shakspeare's heroes rendered by some master that he went, and probably he never was inside a theatre twenty times in his life, and, so sensitive was he to had taste or ranting, that he was usually sorry that had gone.

The rendering of Richard II. (I cannot remember by whom) more than satisfied him, and he liked to recall the actor's tones in reading this play, an especial favorite of his, to his children. Coriolanus and Julius Cæsar too he enjoyed reading to them, and he selected passages from Shakspeare for them and trained them very carefully for their recitation in school.

He saw Edwin Booth in Boston, and met him later at the house of a friend and had some talk with him. Booth later mentioned with pleasure to their host the fact that Mr. Emerson had not once alluded to his profession or performance in their conversation.

Mr. Emerson once defined the cultivated man as "one who can tell you something new and true about Shakspeare." And he read a good omen for our age in Shakspeare's acceptance: "The book only characterizes the reader. Is Shakspeare the delight of the nineteenth century? That fact only shows whereabouts we are in the ecliptic of the soul."

In writing of Great Men in 1838 in his journal, he says:—

"Swedenborg is scarce yet appreciable. Shakspeare has, for the first time, in our time found adequate criticism, if indeed he have yet found it:—Coleridge, Lamb, Schlegel, Goethe, Very, Herder.

"The great facts of history are four or five names, Homer—Phidias—Jesus—Shakspeare. One or two names more I will not add, but see what these names stand for. All civil history and all philosophy consists of endeavours more or less vain to explain these persons."

In the journal for 1843 he writes: "Plato is weak inasmuch as he is literary. Shakspeare is not literary, but the strong earth itself." Yet from another point of view he writes, "Shakspeare and Plato each sufficed for the culture of a nation."

That Shakspeare and Milton should have been born meant much to him and to mankind. "Who saw Milton, who saw Shakspeare, saw them do their best, and utter their whole heart manlike among their contemporaries."

And again, "No man can be named whose mind still acts on the cultivated intellect of England and America with an energy comparable to that of Milton. As a poet, Shakspeare undoubtedly transcends and far surpasses him in his popularity with foreign nations: but Shakspeare is a voice merely: who and what he was that sang, that sings, we know not."

Note 2.

Mr. Emerson said of Nature:—

No ray is dimmed, no atom worn,
My oldest force is good as new,
And the fresh rose on yonder thorn
Gives back the bending heavens in dew;—

and her cheerful lesson for the artist or poet was that he too could forever re-combine the old material into fresh and splendid pictures. He rejoiced that "the poet is permitted to dip his brush into the old paint-pot with which birds, flowers, the human cheek, the living rock, the broad landscape, the ocean and the eternal sky were painted," and turning from the reading of the plays he says: "'T is Shakspeare's fault that the world appears so empty. He has educated you with his painted world, and this real one seems a huckster's-shop." Again as to his true rendering of men's characters, "I value

Shakspeare as a metaphysician and admire the unspoken logic which upholds the structure of Iago, Macbeth, Antony and the rest."

Note 3.

Again the ancient doctrine of the Flowing, and the modern onward and upward stream of Evolution.

Note 4.

*The passive Master lent his hand
To the vast soul that o'er him planned.
"The Problem," Poems.*

Note 5.

The stage was to Shakspeare his opportunity, as the Lyceum was to Emerson.

Note 6.

Henry VIII., Act V., Scene iv.

Note 7.

This estimate of the value of memory to the poet, typified by the Greeks in their making the Muses the daughters of Mnemosyne, is enlarged upon in the Essay on "Memory" in Natural History of Intellect. Mr. Emerson said once, "Of the most romantic fact the memory is more romantic," and he quotes Quintilian as saying, Quantum ingenii, tantum memoriæ.

Note 8.

In a fragment of verse written in Mr. Emerson's journal of 1831 on the yearning of the poet to enrich himself from the Treasury of the Universe, he says:—

*And if to me it is not given
To fetch one ingot thence
Of that unfading gold of Heaven
His merchants may dispense,
Yet well I know the royal mine,*

*And know the sparkle of its ore,
Know Heaven's truth from lies that shine,—*

*Explored, they teach us to explore.
"Fragments on the Poet," Poems, Appendix.*

Note 9.

Milton, "Il Penseroso."

Note 10.

Taine, in his History of English Literature, thus justifies Chaucer's borrowing or rendering:—

"Chaucer was capable of seeking out, in the old common forest of the middle ages, stories and legends, to replant them in his own soil and make them send out new shoots…. He has the right and power of copying and translating because by dint of retouching he impresses … his original mark. He re-creates what he imitates…. At the distance of a century and a half he has affinity with the poets of Elizabeth by his gallery of pictures."

The dates of Lydgate and Caxton show a mistake as to his use of them. Caxton, following Chaucer, when he introduced the printing-press to England, printed his poems and those of Lydgate, who was younger than Chaucer. In his House of Fame, Chaucer places, in his vision, "on a pillar higher than the rest, Homer and Livy, Dares the Phrygian, Guido Colonna, Geoffrey of Monmouth and the other historians of the war of Troy" [Taine's History of English Literature], a due recognition of his debt for Troylus and Cryseyde. As for Gower, he was Chaucer's exact contemporary and friend, and Chaucer dedicated this poem to him.

Note 11.

Kipling irreverently tells of Homer's borrowings thus:—

"When 'Omer smote 'is bloomin' lyre,
He 'd 'eard men sing by land an' sea;
An' what he thought 'e might require,
'E went an' took—the same as me!"
And says of his humble audience:—

"They knew 'e stole; 'e knew they knowed.
They did n't tell, nor make a fuss,
But winked at 'Omer down the road,
An' 'e winked back—the same as us!"

Note 12.

Dr. Holmes's remark with regard to the preceding page is: "The reason why Emerson has so much to say on this subject of borrowing, especially when treating of Plato and Shakspeare, is obvious enough. He was arguing his own cause—not defending himself," etc. In Letters and Social Aims, Mr. Emerson discusses Quotation and Originality.

Note 13.

Mr. Emerson had tender associations with the Book of Common Prayer. His mother had been brought up in the Episcopal communion, and the prayer-book of her youth was always by her, though after her marriage she attended her husband's church. [In Mr. Cabot's Memoir, vol. ii. p. 572, see Mr. Emerson's letter on his mother's death.]

Note 14.

Landor says of these borrowings of Shakspeare, "He breathed upon dead bodies and brought them to life."

Note 15.

The princes Ferrex and Porrex, brothers and rivals for the ancient British throne, are characters in the tragedy Gorboduc by Norton and Sackville, to which the date 1561 is assigned. Gammer Gurton's Needle is a comedy of the same period.

Note 16.

Journal, 1864. "Shakspeare puts us all out. No theory will account for him. He neglected his works, perchance he did not know their value? Ay, but he did; witness the sonnets. He went into company as a listener, hiding himself, [Greek]; was only remembered by all as a delightful companion."

Note 17.

England's genius filled all measure
Of heart and soul, of strength and pleasure,
Gave to the mind its emperor,
And life was larger than before:
Nor sequent centuries could hit
Orbit and sum of Shakspeare's wit.
The men who lived with him became
Poets, for the air was fame.
"The Solution," Poems.

Note 18.

While writing this, Mr. Emerson was surrounded by persons paralyzed for active life in the common world by the doubts of conscience or entangled in over-fine-spun webs of their intellect. [back]

Note 19.

Journal, 1837. "I either read or inferred to-day in the Westminster Review that Shakspeare was not a popular man in his day. How true and wise. He sat alone and walked alone, a visionary poet, and came with his piece, modest but discerning, to the players, and was too glad to get it received, whilst he was too superior not to see its transcendent claims."

Note 20.

The following is the "Exordium of a lecture on Poetry and Eloquence," given in London in 1848:

"Shakspeare is nothing but a large utterance. We cannot find that anything in his age was more worth telling than anything in ours; nor give any account of his existence, but only the fact that there was a wonderful symbolizer and expresser, who has no rival in the ages, and who has thrown an accidental lustre over his time and subject."

In the lecture on "Works and Days" he wrote, "Shakspeare made his Hamlet as a bird weaves its nest." And in that on "Inspiration" in Letters and Social Aims: "Shakspeare seems to you miraculous, but the wonderful juxtapositions, parallelisms, transfers, which his genius effected, were all to him locked together as links of a chain, and the mode precisely as conceivable and familiar to higher intelligence as the index-making of the literary hack."

Journal, 1838. "Read Lear yesterday and Hamlet to-day with new wonder and mused much on the great Soul in the broad continuous daylight of these poems. Especially I wonder at the perfect reception this wit and immense knowledge of life and intellectual superiority find in us all in connection with our utter incapacity to produce anything like it. The superior tone of Hamlet in all the conversations how perfectly preserved, without any mediocrity, much less any dulness in the other speakers.

"How real the loftiness! an inborn gentleman; and above that, an exalted intellect. What incessant growth and plenitude of thought,—pausing on itself never an instant, and each sally of wit sufficient to save the play. How true then and unerring the earnest of the dialogue, as when Hamlet talks with the Queen. How terrible his discourse! What less can be said of the perfect mastery, as by a superior being, of the conduct of the drama, as the free introduction of this capital advice to the players; the commanding good sense which never retreats except before the Godhead which inspires certain passages—the more I think of it, the more I wonder. I will think nothing impossible to man. No Parthenon, no sculpture, no picture, no architecture can be named beside this. All this is perfectly visible to me and to many,—the wonderful truth and mastery of this work, of these works,—yet for our lives could not I, or any man, or all men, produce anything comparable to one scene in Hamlet or Lear. With all my admiration of this life-like picture, set me to producing a match for it, and I should instantly depart into mouthing rhetoric.... One other fact Shakspeare presents us; that not by books are great poets made. Somewhat—and much, he unquestionably owes to his books; but you could not find in his circumstances the history of his poems. It was made without hands in his invisible world. A mightier magic than any learning, the deep logic of cause and effect he studied: its roots were cast so deep, therefore it flung out its branches so high."

Note 21.

Mr. Edwin P. Whipple, writing in Harper's Monthly in 1882, relates how in a long drive with Mr. Emerson, after a lecture, "The conversation at last drifted to contemporary actors who assumed to personate leading characters in Shakspeare's greatest plays. Had I ever seen an actor who satisfied me when he pretended to be Hamlet or Othello, Lear or Macbeth? Yes, I had seen the elder Booth in these characters. Though not perfect, he approached nearer to perfection than any other actor I knew—

"'Ah,' said Emerson, [after] the three minutes I consumed in eulogizing Booth,... 'I see you are one of the happy mortals who are capable of being carried away by an actor of Shakspeare. Now, whenever I visit the theatre to witness the performance of one of his dramas, I am carried away by the poet. I went last Tuesday to see Macready in Hamlet. I got along very well until he came to the passage:—

"thou, dead corse, again, in complete steel,
Revisit'st thus the glimpses of the moon:"—

and then actor, theatre, all vanished in view of that solving and dissolving imagination, which could reduce this big globe and all it inherits into mere "glimpses of the moon." The play went on, but, absorbed in this one thought of the mighty master, I paid no heed to it.'

"What specially impressed me, as Emerson was speaking, was his glance at our surroundings as he slowly uttered, 'glimpses of the moon,' for here above us was the same moon which must have given birth to Shakspeare's thought.... Afterward, in his lecture on Shakspeare, Emerson made use of the thought suggested in our ride by moonlight. He said, 'That imagination which dilates the closet he writes in to the world's dimensions, crowds it with agents in rank and order, as quickly reduces the big reality to be the "glimpses of the moon."'... In the printed lecture, there is one sentence declaring the absolute insufficiency of any actor, in any theatre, to fix attention on himself while uttering Shakspeare's words, which seems to me the most exquisite statement ever made of the magical suggestiveness of Shakspeare's expression. I have often quoted it, but it will bear quotation again and again, as the best prose sentence ever written on this side of the Atlantic: 'The recitation begins; one golden word leaps out immortal from all this painted pedantry, and sweetly torments us with invitations to its own inaccessible homes.'"

Note 22.

The little Shakspeare in the maiden's heart
Makes Romeo of a ploughboy on his cart;
Opens the eye to Virtue's starlike meed
And gives persuasion to a gentle deed.
"The Enchanter," Poems, Appendix.

Note 23.

And yet perhaps there is some truth in Dr. Richard Garnett's word in his Life of Emerson:

"Emerson is incapable of contemplating Shakspeare with the eye of a dramatic critic."

Just after Mr. Emerson settled in Concord he read with great pleasure Henry Taylor's play Philip van Artevelde, then recently published. He wrote in his journal for 1835:—

"I think Taylor's poem is the best light we have ever had upon the genius of Shakspeare. We have made a miracle of Shakspeare, a haze of light instead of a guiding torch, by accepting unquestioned all the tavern stories about his want of education, and total unconsciousness. The internal evidence all the time is irresistible that he was no such person. He was a man, like this Taylor, of strong sense and of great cultivation; an excellent Latin scholar, and of extensive and select reading, so as to have formed his theories of many historical characters with as much clearness as Gibbon or Niebuhr or Goethe. He wrote for intelligent persons, and wrote with intention. He had Taylor's strong good sense, and added to it his own wonderful facility of execution which aerates and sublimes all language the moment he uses it, or more truly, animates every word."

Note 24.

Lowell, in one of his essays, calls attention to the survival in New England of the type of face of the English in Queen Elizabeth's day even more than in the mother country, and also to the old English expressions, obsolete in England, but still current on New England farms.

Note 25.

Journal, 1838. fills us with wonder the first time we approach him. We go away, and work and think, for years, and come again,—he astonishes us anew. Then, having drank deeply and saturated us with his genius, we lose sight of him for another period of years. By and by we return, and there he stands immeasurable as at first. We have grown wiser, but only that we should see him wiser than ever. He resembles a high mountain which the traveller sees in the morning, and thinks he shall quickly near it and pass it, and leave it behind. But he journeys all day till noon, till night. There still is the dim mountain close by him, having scarce altered its bearings since the morning light."

Note 26.

*And yet it seemeth not to me
That the high gods love tragedy;
For Saadi sat in the sun,
And thanks was his contrition;*

*And yet his runes he rightly read,
And to his folk his message sped.*
"Saadi," Poems.

Note 27.

This image appears in "The Apology" in the Poems.

Note 28.

The Puritan shrinking from the form in which the great poet embodied his thought or oracles or dreams still appears in the journal of 1852, yet, contrasted to the dismal seers, Shakspeare is well-nigh pardoned his levity.

"There was never anything more excellent came from a human brain than the plays of Shakspeare, bating only that they were plays. The Greek has a real advantage of them in the degree in which his dramas had a religious office. Could the priest look him in the face without blenching?"

In 1839 Mr. Emerson had written:—

"It is in the nature of things that the highest originality must be moral. The only person who can be entirely independent of this fountain of literature and equal to it, must be a prophet in his own proper person. Shakspeare, the first literary genius of the world, leans on the Bible: his poetry supposes it. If we examine this brilliant influence, Shakspeare, as it lies in our minds, we shall find it reverent, deeply indebted to the traditional morality, in short, compared with the tone of the prophets, Secondary. On the other hand, the Prophets do not imply the existence of Shakspeare or Homer,—to no books or arts,—only to dread Ideas and emotions."

Note 29.

All through his life Mr. Emerson felt increasing thankfulness for "the Spirit of joy which Shakspeare had shed over the Universe." In 1864 he wrote:—

"When I read Shakspeare, as lately, I think the criticism and study of him to be in their infancy. The wonder grows of his long obscurity:—how could you hide the only man that ever wrote from all men who delight in reading?"

And again he wrote: "Your criticism is profane. Shakspeare by Shakspeare. The poet in his interlunation is a critic,"—that is, his worst is criticised by his best performance.

Journal, 1864. "How to say it I know not, but I know that the point of praise of Shakspeare is the pure poetic power: he is the chosen closet companion, who can, at any moment, by incessant surprises, work the miracle of mythologizing every fact of the common life; as snow, or moonlight, or the level rays of sunrise lend a momentary glow to Pump and wood-pile."

And again: 1836. "It is easy to solve the problem of individual existence. Why Milton, Shakspeare, or Canova should be there is reason enough. But why the million should exist drunk with the opium of Time and Custom does not appear."

But even Shakspeare must not be idolized. The soul must rely on itself, that is, on the universal fountain of beauty, wisdom and goodness to which it is open. So thus he draws the moral:—

1838. "The indisposition of men to go back to the source and mix with Deity is the reason of degradation and decay. Education is expended in the measurement and imitation of effects in the study of Shakspeare, for example, as itself a perfect being—instead of using Shakspeare merely as an effect of which the cause is with every scholar. Thus the college becomes idolatrous—a temple full of idols. Shakspeare will never be made by the study of Shakspeare. I know not how directions for greatness can be given, yet greatness may be inspired."

Feb. 1838. "Consider too how Shakspeare and Milton are formed. They are just such men as we all are to contemporaries, and none suspected their superiority,—but after all were dead, and a generation or two besides, it is discovered that they surpass all. Each of us then take the same moral to himself."

William Shakespeare – A Tribute in Verse

Index of Contents
To the Memory of My Beloved, the Author, Mr William Shakespeare, & What He Hath Left Us by Ben Jonson
Shakespeare by Matthew Arnold
An Epitaph On The Admirable Dramatic Poet W. Shakespeare by John Milton
Shakespeare by Henry Wadsworth Longfellow
Elegy On Mr. William Shakespeare by William Basse
Shakespeare by Vachel Lindsay
The Spirit of Shakespeare by George Meredith
To Shakespeare by Lord Alfred Douglas
To Shakespeare (I) by Frances Anne Kemble
To Shakespeare (II) by Frances Anne Kemble
To Shakespeare (III) by Frances Anne Kemble
Shakespeare and Milton by Walter Savage Landor
A Shakespeare Memorial by Alfred Austin
Shakespeare by Mathilde Blind
Shakespeare by Robert Crawford
Shakespeare by Thomas Gent
Shakespeare's Mourners by John Bannister Tabb
Shakespeare by Philip Henry Savage
Shakespeare by Lucretia Maria Davidson
Shakespeare by Frederick George Scott
Shakespeare's Kingdom by Alfred Noyes
Shakespeare 1916 by Sir Ronald Ross
Song, In Imitation of Shakspeare's by James Beattie
In A Letter To C. P. Esq. In Imitation o Shakspeare by William Cowper
Shakspeare. (An Ode For His Three-Hundredth Birthday) by Martin Farquhar Tupper

On The Site of A Mulberry-Tree; Planted By Wm. Shakspeare; Felled By The Rev. F. Gastrell by Dante Gabriel Rossetti

To The Memory of My Beloved, The Author, Mr William Shakespeare, And What He Hath Left Us by Ben Jonson

To draw no envy, Shakespeare, on thy name
Am I thus ample to thy book and fame;
While I confess thy writings to be such
As neither Man nor Muse can praise too much.
'Tis true, and all men's suffrage. But these ways
Were not the paths I meant unto thy praise;
For silliest ignorance on these may light,
Which when it sounds at best but echoes right;
Or blind affection, which doth ne'er advance
The truth, but gropes, and urges all by chance;
Or crafty malice might pretend this praise,
And think to ruin where it seemed to raise.
These are as some infamous bawd or whore
Should praise a matron. What could hurt her more?
But thou art proof against them, and indeed
Above th' ill fortune of them, or the need.
I therefore will begin: Soul of the Age!
The applause, delight, the wonder of our stage!
My Shakespeare, rise; I will not lodge thee by
Chaucer, or Spenser, or bid Beaumont lie
A little further, to make thee a room:
Thou art a monument without a tomb,
And art alive still, while thy book doth live,
And we have wits to read, and praise to give.
That I not mix thee so, my brain excuses,
I mean with great but disproportioned Muses,
For if I thought my judgement were of years,
I should commit thee surely with thy peers,
And tell how far thou didst our Lyly outshine,
Or sporting Kyd, or Marlowe's mighty line.
And though thou hadst small Latin and less Greek,
From thence to honour thee I would not seek
For names; but call forth thundering Aeschylus,
Euripides, and Sophocles to us,
Pacuvius, Accius, him of Cordova dead,
To live again, to hear thy buskin tread,
And shake a stage; or, when thy socks were on,
Leave thee alone for the comparison
Of all that insolent Greece or haughty Rome
Sent forth, or since did from their ashes come.
Triumph, my Britain, thou hast one to show
To whom all scenes of Europe homage owe.
He was not of an age, but for all time!

And all the Muses still were in their prime
When, like Apollo, he came forth to warm
Our ears, or, like a Mercury, to charm!
Nature herself was proud of his designs,
And joyed to wear the dressing of his lines!
Which were so richly spun, and woven so fit,
As, since, she will vouchsafe no other wit.
The merry Greek, tart Aristophanes,
Neat Terence, witty Plautus, now not please;
But antiquated and deserted lie,
As they were not of Nature's family.
Yet must I not give Nature all; thy art,
My gentle Shakespeare, must enjoy a part.
For though the poet's matter nature be,
His art doth give the fashion; and that he
Who casts to write a living line must sweat
(Such as thine are) and strike the second heat
Upon the Muses' anvil; turn the same,
And himself with it, that he thinks to frame,
Or for the laurel he may gain a scorn;
For a good poet's made as well as born.
And such wert thou. Look how the father's face
Lives in his issue, even so the race
Of Shakespeare's mind and manners brightly shines
In his well turned and true-filed lines:
In each of which he seems to shake a lance,
As brandished at the eyes of ignorance.
Sweet swan of Avon! what a sight it were
To see thee in our waters yet appear,
And make those flights upon the banks of Thames,
That did so take Eliza and our James!
But stay, I see thee in the hemisphere
Advanced, and made a constellation there:
Shine forth, thou Star of Poets, and with rage,
Or influence, chide or cheer the drooping stage,
Which, since thy flight from hence, hath mourned like night,
And despairs day, but for thy volume's light.

Shakespeare by Matthew Arnold

Others abide our question. Thou art free.
We ask and ask—Thou smilest and art still,
Out-topping knowledge. For the loftiest hill,
Who to the stars uncrowns his majesty,

Planting his steadfast footsteps in the sea,
Making the heaven of heavens his dwelling-place,
Spares but the cloudy border of his base
To the foil'd searching of mortality;

And thou, who didst the stars and sunbeams know,
Self-school'd, self-scann'd, self-honour'd, self-secure,
Didst tread on earth unguess'd at.—Better so!

All pains the immortal spirit must endure,
All weakness which impairs, all griefs which bow,
Find their sole speech in that victorious brow

An Epitaph On The Admirable Dramatic Poet W. Shakespeare by John Milton

What needs my Shakespeare for his honored bones
The labor of an age in piled stones?
Or that his hallowed reliques should be hid
Under a star-ypointing pyramid?
Dear son of Memory, great heir of Fame,
What need'st thou such weak witness of thy name?
Thou in our wonder and astonishment
Hast built thy self a livelong monument.
For whilst, to th' shame of slow-endeavoring art,
Thy easy numbers flow, and that each heart
Hath from the leaves of thy unvalued book
Those Delphic lines with deep impression took,
Then thou, our fancy of itself bereaving,
Dost make us marble with too much conceiving,
And so sepulchred in such pomp dost lie
That kings for such a tomb would wish to die.

Shakespeare by Henry Wadsworth Longfellow

A vision as of crowded city streets,
With human life in endless overflow;
Thunder of thoroughfares; trumpets that blow
To battle; clamor, in obscure retreats,
Of sailors landed from their anchored fleets;
Tolling of bells in turrets, and below
Voices of children, and bright flowers that throw
O'er garden-walls their intermingled sweets!
This vision comes to me when I unfold
The volume of the Poet paramount,
Whom all the Muses loved, not one alone;—
Into his hands they put the lyre of gold,
And, crowned with sacred laurel at their fount,
Placed him as Musagetes on their throne.

Elegy On Mr. William Shakespeare by William Basse

Renowned Spenser, lie a thought more nigh
To learned Chaucer, and rare Beaumont lie
A little nearer Spenser, to make room
For Shakespeare in your threefold, fourfold tomb.
To lodge all four in one bed, make a shift
Until Doomsday, for hardly will a fift
Betwixt this day and that by Fate be slain,
For whom your curtains may be drawn again.
If your precedency in death doth bar
A fourth place in your sacred sepulchre,
Under this carved marble of thine own,
Sleep, rare tragedian, Shakespeare, sleep alone;
Thy unmolested peace, unshared cave
Possess as lord, not tenant of thy grave,
That unto us and others it may be
Honour hereafter to be laid by thee.

Shakespeare by Vachel Lindsay

Would that in body and spirit Shakespeare came
Visible emperor of the deeds of Time,
With Justice still the genius of his rhyme,
Giving each man his due, each passion grace,
Impartial as the rain from Heaven's face
Or sunshine from the heaven-enthroned sun.
Sweet Swan of Avon, come to us again.
Teach us to write, and writing, to be men.

The Spirit of Shakespeare by George Meredith

Thy greatest knew thee, Mother Earth; unsoured
He knew thy sons. He probed from hell to hell
Of human passions, but of love deflowered
His wisdom was not, for he knew thee well.
Thence came the honeyed corner at his lips,
The conquering smile wherein his spirit sails
Calm as the God who the white sea-wave whips,
Yet full of speech and intershifting tales,
Close mirrors of us: thence had he the laugh
We feel is thine: broad as ten thousand beeves
At pasture! thence thy songs, that winnow chaff
From grain, bid sick Philosophy's last leaves
Whirl, if they have no response-they enforced
To fatten Earth when from her soul divorced.

To Shakespeare by Lord Alfred Douglas

Most tuneful singer, lover tenderest,
Most sad, most piteous, and most musical,
Thine is the shrine more pilgrim-worn than all
The shrines of singers; high above the rest
Thy trumpet sounds most loud, most manifest.
Yet better were it if a lonely call
Of woodland birds, a song, a madrigal,
Were all the jetsam of thy sea's unrest.

For now thy praises have become too loud
On vulgar lips, and every yelping cur
Yaps thee a paean; the whiles little men,
Not tall enough to worship in a crowd,
Spit their small wits at thee. Ah! better then
The broken shrine, the lonely worshipper.

To Shakespeare (I) by Frances Anne Kemble

If from the height of that celestial sphere
Where now thou dwell'st, spirit powerful and sweet!
Thou yet canst love the race that sojourn here,
How must thou joy, with pleasure not unmeet
For thy exalted state, to know how dear
Thy memory is held throughout the earth,
Beyond the favoured land that gave thee birth.
E'en in thy seat in Heaven, thou may'st receive
Thanks, praise, and love, and wonder ever new,
From human hearts, who in thy verse perceive
All that humanity calls good and true;
Nor dost thou for each mortal blemish grieve,
They from thy glorious works have fall'n away,
As from thy soul its outward form of clay.

To Shakespeare (II) by Frances Anne Kemble

Oft, when my lips I open to rehearse
Thy wondrous spells of wisdom and of power,
And that my voice and thy immortal verse
On listening ears and hearts I mingled pour,
I shrink dismayed—and awful doth appear
The vain presumption of my own weak deed;
Thy glorious spirit seems to mine so near,
That suddenly I tremble as I read—

Thee an invisible auditor I fear:
Oh, if it might be so, my master dear!
With what beseeching would I pray to thee,
To make me equal to my noble task,
Succour from thee, how humbly would I ask,
Thy worthiest works to utter worthily.

To Shakespeare (III) by Frances Anne Kemble

Shelter and succour such as common men
Afford the weaker partners of their fate,
Have I derived from thee—from thee, most great
And powerful genius! whose sublime control,
Still from thy grave governs each human soul,
That reads the wondrous records of thy pen.
From sordid sorrows thou hast set me free,
And turned from want's grim ways my tottering feet,
And to sad empty hours, given royally,
A labour, than all leisure far more sweet:
The daily bread, for which we humbly pray,
Thou gavest me as if I were thy child,
And still with converse noble, wise, and mild,
Charmed from despair my sinking soul away;
Shall I not bless the need, to which was given
Of all the angels in the host of heaven,
Thee, for my guardian, spirit strong and bland!
Lord of the speech of my dear native land!

Shakespeare and Milton by Walter Savage Landor

The tongue of England, that which myriads
Have spoken and will speak, were paralyz'd
Hereafter, but two mighty men stand forth
Above the flight of ages, two alone;
One crying out,
All nations spoke through me.
The other:
True; and through this trumpet burst God's word;
The fall of Angels, and the doom
First of immortal, then of mortal, Man.
Glory! be glory! not to me, to God.

A Shakespeare Memorial by Alfred Austin

Why should we lodge in marble or in bronze

Spirits more vast than earth, or sea, or sky?
Wiser the silent worshipper that cons
Their words for wisdom that will never die.
Unto the favourite of the passing hour
Erect the statue and parade the bust;
Whereon decisive Time will slowly shower
Oblivion's refuse and disdainful dust.
The Monarchs of the Mind, self-sceptred Kings,
Need no memento to transmit their name:
Throned on their thoughts and high imaginings,
They are the Lords, not sycophants of Fame.
Raise pedestals to perishable stuff:
Gods for themselves are monuments enough.

Shakespeare by Mathilde Blind

Yearning to know herself for all she was,
Her passionate clash of warring good and ill,
Her new life ever ground in Death's old mill,
With every delicate detail and en masse,—
Blind Nature strove. Lo, then it came to pass,
That Time, to work out her unconscious Will,
Once wrought the Mind which she had groped for still,
And she beheld herself as in a glass.

The world of men, unrolled before our sight,
Showed like a map, where stream and waterfall
And village-cradling vale and cloud-capped height
Stand faithfully recorded, great and small;
For Shakespeare was, and at his touch, with light
Impartial as the Sun's, revealed the All.

Shakespeare by Robert Crawford

And what think ye of Shakespeare? 'Twas not he
Of Stratford is the lord of England's lyre;
Ay, not the rustic lad, whoe'er it be,
Momentous in his doing and desire.
But little Latin and less Greek? Ah, no!
It was a teeming scholar who enwrought
The wondrous pages where the wisest go
For th' culmination of the life of thought.
No jovial actor, no mere Shakescene who
Found it so hard his dear name to indite,
The marvellous pictures of our nature drew
And limned the universe in his delight.
We do not know the man; but 'twas not Will

Whose hand is on the lyre of England still.

Shakespeare by Thomas Gent

While o'er this pageant of sublunar things
Oblivion spreads her unrelenting wings,
And sweeps adown her dark unebbing tide
Man, and his mightiest monuments of pride-
Alone, aloft, immutable, sublime,
Star-like, ensphered above the track of time,
Great SHAKSPEARE beams with undiminish'd ray.
His bright creations sacred from decay,
Like Nature's self, whose living form he drew,
Though still the same, still beautiful and new.

He came, untaught in academic bowers,
A gift to Glory from the Sylvan powers:
But what keen Sage, with all the science fraught,
By elder bards or later critics taught,
Shall count the cords of his mellifluous shell,
Span the vast fabric of his fame, and tell
By what strange arts he bade the structure rise-
On what deep site the strong foundation lies?
This, why should scholiasts labour to reveal?
We all can answer it, we all can feel,
Ten thousand sympathies, attesting, start-
For SHAKSPEARE'S Temple, is the human heart!

Lord of a throne which mortal ne'er shall share-
Despot adored! he rales and revels there.
Who but has found, where'er his track hath been,
Through life's oft shifting, multifarious scene,
Still at his side the genial Bard attend,
His loved companion, counsellor, and friend!

The Thespian Sisters nurtured in the schools
Of Greece and Rome, and long coerced by rules,
Scarce moved the inmates of their native hearth
With tiny pathos and with trivial mirth,
Till She, great muse of daring enterprise,
Delighted ENGLAND! saw her SHAKSPEARE rise!

Then, first aroused in that appointed hour,
The Tragic Muse confess'd th' inspiring power;
Sudden before the startled earth she stood,
A giant spectre, weeping tears and blood;
Guilt shrunk appall'd, Despair embraced his shroud,
And Terror shriek'd, and Pity sobb'd aloud;-
Then, first Thalia with dilated ken

And quicken'd footstep pierced the walks of men;
Then Folly blush'd, Vice fled the general hiss,
Delight met Reason with a loving kiss;
At Satire's glance Pride smooth'd his low'ring crest,
The Graces weaved the dance.-And last and best
Came Momus down in Falstaff's form to earth.
To make the world one universe of mirth!

Such Sympathies the glorious Bard endear!
Thus fair he walks in Man's diurnal sphere.
But when, upborne on bright Invention's wings.
He dares the realms of uncreated things,
Forms more divine, more dreadful, start to view,
Than ever Hades or Olympus knew.
Round the dark cauldron, terrible and fell,
The midnight Witches breathe the songs of hell;
Delighted Ariel wings his fiery way
To whirl the storm, the wheeling Orbs to stay;
Then bathes in honey-dews, and sleeps in flowers;
Meanwhile, young Oberon, girt with shadowy powers,
Pursues o'er Ocean's verge the pale cold Moon,
Or hymns her, riding in her highest noon.

Thus graced, thus glorified, shall SHAKSPEARE crave
The Sculptor's skill, the pageant of the grave?
HE needs it not-but Gratitude demands
This votive offering at his Country's hands.
Haply, e'er now, from blissful bowers on high,
From some Parnassus of the empyreal sky,
Pleased, o'er this dome the gentle Spirit bends,
Accepts the gift, and hails us as his friends-
Yet smiles, perchance, to think when envious Time
O'er Bust and Urn shall bid his ivies climb,
When Palaces and Pyramids shall fall-
HIS PAGE SHALL TRIUMPH-still surviving all-
'Till Earth itself, 'like breath upon the wind,'
Shall melt away, 'nor leave a rack behind!'

Shakespeare's Mourners by John Bannister Tabb

I saw the grave of Shakespeare in a dream,
And round about it grouped a wondrous throng,
His own majestic mourners, who belong
Forever to the Stage of Life, and seem
The rivals of reality. Supreme
Stood Hamlet, as erewhile the graves among,
Mantled in thought: and sad Ophelia sung
The same swan-dirge she chanted in the stream.
Othello, dark in destiny's eclipse,

Laid on the tomb a lily. Near him wept
Dejected Constance. Fair Cordelia's lips
Moved prayerfully the while her father slept,
And each and all, inspired of vital breath,
Kept vigil o'er the sacred spoils of death.

Shakespeare by Philip Henry Savage

Through time untimed, if truly great, a Name
Reverence compels and, that forgotten, shame.
But in the stress of living you shall scan,
Yea, touch and censure, great or small, the Man.

Shakespeare by Lucretia Maria Davidson

Shakspeare!' with all thy faults, (and few have more,)
I love thee still,' and still will con thee o'er.
Heaven, in compassion to man's erring heart,
Gave thee of virtue — then, of vice a part,
Lest we, in wonder here, should bow before thee,
Break God's commandment, worship, and adore thee:
But admiration now, and sorrow join;
His works we reverence, while we pity thine.

Shakespeare by Frederick George Scott

Unseen in the great minister dome of time,
Whose shafts are centuries, its spangled roof
The vaulted universe, our master sits,
And organ-voices like a far-off chime
Roll thro' the aisles of thought. The sunlight flits

From arch to arch, and, as he sits aloof,
Kings, heroes, priests, in concourse vast, sublime,
Glances of love and cries from battle-field,
His wizard power breathes on the living air.
Warm faces gleam and pass, child, woman, man,

In the long multitude; but he, concealed,
Our bard eludes us, vainly each face we scan,
It is not he; his features are not there;
But, being thus hid, his greatness is revealed.

Shakespeare's Kingdom by Alfred Noyes

When Shakespeare came to London
He met no shouting throngs;
He carried in his knapsack
A scroll of quiet songs.

No proud heraldic trumpet
Acclaimed him on his way;
Their court and camp have perished;
The songs live on for ay.

Nobody saw or heard them,
But, all around him there,
Spirits of light and music
Went treading the April air.

He passed like any pedlar,
Yet he had wealth untold.
The galleons of th' armada
Could not contain his gold.

The kings rode on to darkness.
In England's conquering hour,
Unseen arrived her splendour;
Unknown, her conquering power.

Shakespeare 1916 by Sir Ronald Ross

Now when the sinking Sun reeketh with blood,
And the gore-gushing vapors rent by him
Rend him and bury him: now the World is dim
As when great thunders gather for the flood,
And in the darkness men die where they stood,
And dying slay, or scatter'd limb from limb
Cease in a flash where mad-eyed cherubim
Of Death destroy them in the night and mud:
When landmarks vanish—murder is become
A glory—cowardice, conscience— and to lie,
A law—to govern, but to serve a time:—
We dying, lifting bloodied eyes and dumb,
Behold the silver star serene on high,
That is thy spirit there, O Master Mind sublime.

Song, In Imitation of Shakspeare's by James Beattie

I

Blow, blow, thou vernal gale!
Thy balm will not avail
To ease my aching breast;
Though thou the billows smooth,
Thy murmurs cannot soothe
My weary soul to rest.

II
Flow, flow, thou tuneful stream!
Infuse the easy dream
Into the peaceful soul;
But thou canst not compose
The tumult of my woes,
Though soft thy waters roll.

III
Blush, blush, ye fairest flowers!
Beauties surpassing yours
My Rosalind adorn;
Nor is the Winter's blast,
That lays your glories waste,
So killing as her scorn.

IV
Breathe, breathe, ye tender lays,
That linger down the maze
Of yonder winding grove;
O let your soft control
Bend her relenting soul
To pity and to love.

V
Fade, fade, ye flowerets fair!
Gales, fan no more the air!
Ye streams, forget to glide;
Be hush'd each vernal strain;
Since nought can soothe my pain,
Nor mitigate her pride.

In A Letter To C. P. Esq. In Imitation Of Shakspeare by William Cowper

Trust me the meed of praise, dealt thriftily
From the nice scale of judgement, honours more
Than does the lavish and o'erbearing tide
Of profuse courtesy. Not all the gems
Of India's richest soil at random spread
O'er the gay vesture of some glittering dame,
Give such alluring vantage to the person,
As the scant lustre of a few, with choice

And comely guise of ornament disposed.

Shakspeare. (An Ode For His Three-Hundredth Birthday) by Martin Farquhar Tupper

I.
Immortal! risen to thy Rest,
Immortal! throned among the Blest,
Immortal! long an heir sublime
Of realms outreaching space and time,—
How shall we dare, or hope, to raise
A fitting homage of high praise
To please thy Spirit, sphered on high
Where planets roll and comets fly?
How may not thy pure fame be marr'd
By the damp breath of earthly bard,
Presuming in his zeal too bold
To gild the bright refinèd gold?
Or how canst thou, fill'd with God's love,
And tranced among the saints above,
Endure that men should seem and be
Idolaters in praise of thee!
Forgive our love, forgive our zeal,—
We cannot guess how spirits feel;
And may our homage offered thus
Please HIM who made both thee, and us!

II.
Immortal also on this darker Earth
As in those brighter spheres,
Now will we consecrate our Shakespeare's birth,
This day three hundred years!
And so from age to age for evermore
His glory shall extend,
With men of every land the wide world o'er,
Till Time itself shall end!
For, he is our's; and well with pride and joy
England may bless her son,
The Stratford scholar and the Warwick boy
That every crown hath won!
Let others boast their wisest and their best,
To each a prize may fall;
Genius gives one apiece to all the rest,
But Shakspeare claims them all!

III.
A Homer, in majestic eloquence,
A Terence, for keen wit and stinging sense,
Brighter than Pindar in his loftiest flight,
Darker than Æschylus for deeds of night,

An Ovid, in the story-pictured page,
A Juvenal, to lash the vicious age,
Graceful as Horace and more skill'd to please,
Tender as pity-stirring Sophocles,
Free as Anacreon, as Martial neat,
Than Virgil's self more delicately sweet,—
O let those ancients bend before Thee now,
And pile their many chaplets on one brow!—
Milton was great, and of divinest song,
Spenser melodious, Chaucer rough and strong,—
The vigorous Dryden, and the classic Gray,
And awful Danté, soaring far away,
Schiller and Göethe, stirring up the strife,
And Molière, dropping laughter into life,
Burns, a full spring of nature, Hood of wit,
And Tennyson, most rare and exquisite,
To each and all belongs the laurell'd crown,
And woe to him who drags their honours down,—
Yet, Shakspeare, thou wert all these lights combined,
O manysided crystal of mankind!

IV.
The jealous Moor, the thoughtful Dane,
The witty rare fat knight,
And grand old Lear half-insane,
And fell Iago's spite,
And Romeo's love, and Tybalt's hate,
And Bolinbroke in regal state,
And he that murdered sleep,—
And ruthless Shylock's bloody bond,
And Prosper with his broken wand
Long buried fathoms deep!
Frank Juliet too,— and that soft pair
Helen and Hermia, lilies fair
As growing on one stem,
Love-crazed Ophelia, drown'd ah! drown'd,
And wanton Cleopatra, crown'd
With Egypt's diadem;
The young Miranda most admired,
Cordelia's filial heart,
Sly Beatrice with wit inspired,
And Ariel's tricksey part,
Fair Rosalind,— sweet banishèd,
And gentle Desdemona — dead!—
Ay these, all these, and crowds beside,
Heroes, jesters, courtiers, clowns,
Girls in grief, or kings in pride,
Threats and crimes, and jokes, and frowns,
Witches, fairies, ghosts, and elves,
All our fancies, all ourselves,—
O! thou hast pictured with thy pen

All phases of all hearts of men,
And in thy various page survives
The Panorama of our lives!

V.
O Paragon unthought before,
O miracle of selftaught lore,
A universe of wit and worth,
The admirable Man of earth,
There is nor thing, nor thought, nor whim,
Untouch'd and unadorn'd by him;
No theme unsung, no truth untold
Of Earth's museum, new or old:
All Nature's hidden things he saw,
Intuitive to every law;
Glancing with supernal scan
At all the knowledge spelt by man;
While, for each rule and craft of Art
He grasp'd it amply, whole and part:
Like travel-wise Ulysses well he knew
Peoples and cities, men and manners too;
With shrewd but ever charitable ken
He read, and wrote out fair, the hearts of men;
Yet, in self-knowledge vers'd, a sage outright,
His giant soul was humble in its might!
O gentle, happy, modest mind,
O genial, cheerful, frank and kind,
Not even could domestic strife
Sour the sweetness of thy life,—
But wheresoe'er thy foot might roam,
Divorced from that Xantipp'd home,
Friends ever found thee,— ay, and foes,
Cordial to these, and kind to those;
Brave, loving, patient, generous, just, and good,—
Beloved by all, our matchless Shakspeare stood!

VI.
Where are thy glorious works unknown?
Who hath not heard thy fame?
On every shore, in every zone,
The World, with glad acclaim,
Yea, from the cottage to the throne,
Hath magnified thy name!
From far Australia to Vancouver's pines,
From the High Alps to Russia's deepest mines,
From China, with her English lesson learnt,
To Chili, wailing for her daughters burnt;
There, everywhere, our Shakspeare breathes and moves
In the sweet ether of all human loves!—
Where rent America now writhes in woe,
Where Nile and Danube, Thames and Ganges flow,

Wherever England sails, and human kind
Anywhere feels in heart, and thinks in mind,
There, everywhere, our Shakspeare's voice is heard,
By him all souls are thrill'd, and cheer'd, and stirr'd;
Each passion flows or ebbs, as Shakspeare speaks,
Hate knits the brow, or terror pales the cheeks,
Love lights the eyes, or pity melts the heart,
And all men bow beneath our Poet's art!

VII.
What monument to rear,
What worthy offering?—
Nought lacks thy glory here
Of all thy sons can bring:
Long since, a twin-sphered brother spake,
How vain it were to raise
To such a Name, for Memory's sake,
Its pyramid of praise:
Our Shakspeare needs no sculptured stones,
No temple for his honoured bones!
But haply in his native street
Beside the rescued home
Hallowed by his infant feet
Whereto all pilgrims roam,
A College well might rear its head,
That Townsman's name to bear,
And brother-actors' sons he bred
To light and learning there!
And, for great London and its throngs,—
To Shakspeare of old right belongs
The Shakspeare Bridge, with Shakspeare scenes
Sculptured upon its pannell'd screens,
Colossus-like the Thames to span,
And telling every passing man
Where a poor player in his youth
Served Heaven and Earth by mimic truth,
And wrapped in Art's and Nature's robe,
Leased,— 'twas his Heritage, — the Globe!—

VIII.
Great Magician for all time,
Denizen of every clime,
Darling poet of mankind,
Master of the human mind,
Nature's very priest and king,—
Take the gifts thy children bring!
Let thy Spirit, hovering o'er
Thine earthly home and haunts of yore,
In its wisdom, wealth, and worth,
Shine upon us from above,
While thy kinsmen here on earth

Thus with pious care and love
Celebrate our Shakspeare's birth.

On The Site of A Mulberry-Tree; Planted By Wm. Shakspeare; Felled By The Rev. F. Gastrell by Dante Gabriel Rossetti

This tree, here fall'n, no common birth or death
Shared with its kind. The world's enfranchised son,
Who found the trees of Life and Knowledge one,
Here set it, frailer than his laurel-wreath.
Shall not the wretch whose hand it fell beneath
Rank also singly—the supreme unhung?
Lo! Sheppard, Turpin, pleading with black tongue
This viler thief's unsuffocated breath!
We'll search thy glossary, Shakspeare! whence almost,
And whence alone, some name shall be reveal'd
For this deaf drudge, to whom no length of ears
Sufficed to catch the music of the spheres;
Whose soul is carrion now,—too mean to yield
Some Starveling's ninth allotment of a ghost.

www.ingramcontent.com/pod-product-compliance
Lightning Source LLC
Chambersburg PA
CBHW071504040426
42444CB00008B/1494